SOPHIE GRIGSON'S
FEASTS FOR A FIVER

**For the ballerina and the baker,
from the very intelligent stegosaurus.**

This book is published to accompany
the television series *Sophie Grigson's Feasts for a Fiver,*
which was first broadcast in 1999.
The series was produced by BBC Birmingham.

Executive Producer: Roger Casstles
Producer: Sara Kozak
Assistant Producer: Sue Watson
Directors: Micci Billinger and Lynda Maher

Published by BBC Worldwide Ltd,
80 Wood Lane, London W12 0TT

First published 1999
© Sophie Grigson 1999
The moral right of the author has been asserted.

Photography © Jess Koppel 1999

ISBN 0 563 55110 0

Commissioning Editor: Vivien Bowler
Project Editor: Sally Potter
Text Design: Andrew Barron & Collis Clements Associates
Home Economist: Lyn Rutherford
Stylist: Roisin Nield

Set in Baskerville, Swiss and Akzidenz Grotesk
Printed and bound in France by Imprimerie Pollina s.a.

Colour separations by Imprimerie Pollina s.a.
Jacket printed by Imprimerie Pollina s.a.

#5

Acknowledgements

Making a television series and producing a book involve enormous amounts of work and dedication on the part of a considerable number of people. For most of them it is their job, but there is a select group of people who may come into the process unaware of the demands that it will make on them. In this particular case we took over the homes and lives of six sets of contributors, who rallied round marvellously and good humouredly, despite the lock, stock and barrel intrusion. I would particularly like to thank Harriet Festing, Kumar Vasanthakumar and their daughters, Molly and Daisy, in Kent; Dawn Frost and the Marwood ladies in Devon; Helena, Brenda and Walter, Pastor Chris Watson and the entire congregation of the Kenyon Baptist Church in Brixton; Norah, Ralph and Jennifer Brown in Northern Ireland; Neil, Paul, Rory, Louise and Craig in Leicester; and Fiona and Stephen West, with Amy, Ailsa, Rosina and the utterly edible Moray in Glasgow, for their fortitude and patience.

They may just be doing their jobs but I've had a ball working with the fabulous production team from the BBC – Sara Kozak, so laidback, Lynda Maher and Micci Billinger, directors de luxe, Claire Walls and Oliver Clarke, the enthusiastic researchers whose performance with naan breads was outstanding, and all who worked on the series. Annabel Hartog and Anne Ronald slaved away tirelessly, usually in makeshift kitchens, to prepare food that always looked and tasted splendid. A special thank you to Her Royal Gorgeousness, Sue Watson, and the Eagle-Eyed Jo Garner, despite the fact that they both abandoned the series on the pathetic excuse that they were just about to give birth (and congratulations on two bonny babies). But that's enough about TV. On the book front, I'd like to thank my editor, Viv Bowler, and Sally Potter, for coping with the piecemeal delivery of the manuscript (and look, Viv – only 8 recipes over 100). Jane Middleton, once again, ironed out a multitude of glitches and oversights. My appreciation of my dear friend Jess Koppel increases with each project we work on. Her photographs get more and more beautiful and the food looks, as always, wonderfully appetizing. This is also due to the talented hands and the enthusiasm of food stylist Lyn Rutherford and props stylist Roisin Nield.

In the relative peace of home, I owe an enormous debt of gratitude to Jennine Bierton (soon to be Jennine Hughes – congratulations) for loving and caring for the ballerina and baker with such dedication, and for keeping the house running. Michèle, as always, keeps paperwork at bay and imposes order where there is none. Annabel Hartog, again, and Wendy Malpass have shopped, cooked and tasted enthusiastically, taking charge of the kitchen when paperwork took charge of me, despite Michèle's best efforts. And a special message of thanks to wee Charlie, who does very little but smile and gurgle when he visits, which is more than enough to entertain us all.

Contents

Introduction 5

Cook's Notes 9

SUMMER

1   A Spicy Supper for Four 13

2   A Seaside Lunch for Four 15

3   A Family Picnic for Four to Six 17

4   A Student Lunch for Four 20

5   Supper for Two on the Balcony 25

6   A Working Lunch for Two 25

7   The Marwood Teas 33

8   Midsummer Italian Menu for Two 39

9   Fresh-as-a-daisy Menu for Four 44

10 Saving the Sunshine 47

AUTUMN

1   A Light Lunch for the Workers (for Four) 53

2   A Taste of the Caribbean for Four 57

3   A Harvest Feast for Eight to Ten 60

4   Saturday Supper in the Kitchen for Four 69

5   Sunday Lunch for Four 69

6   Norah's Breads 77

7   Stashing Away the Harvest 79

8   The Comfort Zone – Warming Food for Four 84

WINTER

1   A Light Bright Lunch for Four 89

2   East-meets-West Birthday Banquet for Six 91

3   Size Does Matter – Menu for Four 104

4   Poor Man's Revenge – Menu for Two 106

5   Know Your Onions – Menu for Four 109

6   Menu for a Cold Winter's Day (for Four) 116

7   A Devilishly Good Supper for Four 118

8   Two Classic Winter Preserves 121

SPRING

1   After School Meal for Four 129

2   A Family Supper for Six 131

3   Menu for a Musical Evening (for Four) 136

4   The Call-of-the-wild Menu (for Four) 141

5   Annabel's Spring Menu for Four 144

6   Two Times Two – An Asparagus and Rhubarb Double Bill for Four: Menu I 149

7   Two Times Two – An Asparagus and Rhubarb Double Bill for Four: Menu 2 149

Seasonal Produce 157

A Handful of Useful Addresses 158

Index 159

Introduction

Let me be honest with you from the start. When I began work on this book and the television series it accompanies, I was very anxious about the whole project. It's one thing to come up with delicious ideas for using, say, herbs or vegetables, but being limited by a strict £5 ingredient budget seemed a much more terrifying and testing prospect. Ahead of me lay the Herculean task, or so I thought, of conjuring up a hundred or so recipes that combined strict economy with great tastes. Or, in other words, a collection of menus for entire meals that tasted so good that no one who ate them would dream of accusing their creator of penny-pinching. Do you wonder at my trepidation?

We kicked off in Kent, in watery July sunshine, with all the bounty of the Garden of England at its very best. Inspiring? Well, of course it was, with marvellous summer fruit and vegetables going for a song in a local farm shop, fresh fish from the coast, and beautiful countryside to boot. From there on, there has been no looking back. What started off as an awesome undertaking matured into an exciting challenge, and the possibilities opened up. I jotted down ideas as they occurred – in supermarkets, farm shops, delis and small specialist stores, in my kitchen and in the disordered chaos of my larder. Soon a new and altogether benign problem raised its friendly head – an overabundance of possibilities, endless, enticing and exciting. I still have sheets of potential recipes, as promising in terms of comestibility as they are in terms of cost, lingering untouched and unexplored. There just wasn't room to fit them all in. With great regret I've had to abandon mackerel gravad lax,

Filipino-style pork cooked long and slow, potato gnocchi, marrow and ginger jam, sweet soufflé omelettes oozing sticky, honeyed coconut jam, spring vegetable lasagne and more – volume two in the making, perhaps? My initial concern that I would end up with an overload of pasta dishes has metamorphosed to the opposite extreme: I would like to have included more, but that would have meant leaving out other equally good but less obvious recipes. And so it goes.

What at first seemed daunting turned into a prolific fount of enthusiasm. The moral of the story being that, when it comes to food, low cost does not necessarily mean low quality. I'm lucky enough to have had time to focus on ways to cut costs without cutting corners – or at least not those that matter – and, even more to the point, without cutting the pleasures that a good meal can bring to those who cook it and eat it. In *Feasts for a Fiver*, I am trying to pass on some of what I've learnt over the past few months, and throughout my adult life.

When I first had to cook for myself, for a year in London after I left school, and then as a student in Manchester, I lived on a very tight budget. I may frequently have been strapped for cash but the one thing I wasn't prepared to compromise on was food. It didn't have to be grand but it did have to be good. Armed with Katherine Whitehorn's *Cooking in a Bedsitter*, Jocasta Innes' *The Pauper's Cookbook* and Jack Santa Maria's *Indian Vegetarian Cooking*, I sallied out to markets and small ethnic shops, exploring and feeling my way towards the best that they had to offer. Though my circumstances are very different now, old habits die hard. I still love to rummage around in the Indian food store in my local town; even better, when filming this series I discovered the fabulous market in Leicester, less than an hour's drive away on a good run, and its 'golden mile' at the heart of the town's Asian community. The prices are impressive, the produce superb, the potential thrilling. I returned home laden with sensational white sprouting broccoli (a big thing in Leicester for its all-too-brief three-week season in March), bags of spices, massive bunches of fresh coriander, mint and fenugreek, and many more choice items.

One thing is certain when you are cooking on a budget and that is that you will have to put in a little more effort. Shopping wisely and thriftily is more time consuming than whizzing round the nearest supermarket and grabbing whatever takes your fancy, regardless of price. If your outlay is limited, you will have to work harder at planning menus and meals. You will also have to be prepared to dedicate a little more time to preparation and, possibly, cooking. Heavily packaged convenience foods are out, fresh seasonal produce and cleverly chosen storecupboard supplies are in. The end result is that you may end up eating better than others who pay more money and make less effort. Lobster and caviar are for daydreams, but then who wants them day in, day out? For supper tonight, I'd be more than happy with grilled lamb chops with garlic jam and chickpea mash, or a pearl barley and mushroom risotto, at a fraction of the price.

Seasons

The first principles of any cook who cares about the quality of the food they prepare in their own home are to buy what is best and most abundant in the shops and to grow as much of their fruit, vegetables and herbs as they can themselves, or at least beg or barter from someone else who does. If you stick to this maxim you will not only end up with

deliciously fresh, seasonal produce but you will also save money. When money – or rather lack of it – is an issue, making the most of what is plentiful and cheap or, even better, free, is crucial.

Learn to ignore the ranks of imported strawberries, blueberries, green beans, new potatoes and others that pad out the fresh produce shelves of supermarkets for most of the year. Quite apart from price, they rarely taste as good as fruit and vegetables that are home-grown and in season.

You may not be able to afford the very first British asparagus or strawberries of the year, but wait a week or two until the season is in full swing and the prices will drop to an affordable level even for something that is rated a luxury. Even better than price-watching in the local supermarket or greengrocer's, take a trip to a farm shop or pick-your-own, where the value for money is outstanding and the produce is likely to have been plucked from the ground or bush only a matter of hours earlier. You will be able to savour the difference in every economical mouthful. How smug and superior you will feel then!

Shopping

Shop around and use your common sense. We tend to assume – indeed, we've been led to believe – that supermarkets are the cheapest places to shop. In many instances that's true, but not always. And of course, there are supermarkets and supermarkets. The really, really cheap ones, those 'pile 'em high and sell 'em low' joints, do indeed offer items at breathtakingly low prices but the range is severely limited and the quality of the produce cannot possibly be of the better order. Still, for a few basics such as tinned tomatoes, plain flour, onions and the like, they may be worth an occasional trip if you happen to be in the vicinity.

Far better value for money is the middle rung of supermarkets that offer low prices but a much wider range of items. Don't dismiss the upper echelons of the supermarket ladder altogether in attempts to reduce the weekly bills. For more modern, fashionable ingredients, such as mascarpone or rocket, they can often be cheaper than others, since they sell a greater volume of these things.

Anyone with shopping savvy will, of course, head for the markets. Sadly, many markets in this country are concerned entirely with price, at the expense of quality. Cheap is not necessarily good value for money when the goods are second or third rate. I'm glad to say, however, that there still exist small markets, and some large ones, that preserve the Continental ethos: good prices of course but, far more importantly, high quality, very fresh local produce, picked or plucked within 24 hours of being sold. So unless you are very lucky, you will have to pick and choose wisely in a market. Towards the end of the day (and this happens, too, in supermarkets, particularly on Saturday or Sunday) prices may be slashed to sell off excess goods that will not keep, so this is a good time to go shopping as long as: a) you check what you are buying carefully to make sure that it is not damaged or sub-standard; b) you check sell-by dates or other indicators to make sure that you can use it up in time; and c) you are prepared to take the risk that they may have run out of a number of things that are on your shopping list.

Buying in bulk brings down price but is only worth doing if you will genuinely use everything up before it goes off, or if you can share it with friends or barter it for other foods.

Turn a trip to a pick-your-own farm into a family or friends outing and you are quids in. Choose a sunny day and head off for the fields armed with sunhats, bottles of sun lotion and drinking water. Go for broke and pick enough fruit for jams and jellies (as long as you can find the time to make

them, that is) and enough vegetables for chutneys and relishes. If you have a freezer, stash what you can in it in small packages, ready to use.

Keep an eye out, particularly if you live in the country, for producers who are selling off their second-grade produce at low price. The big buyers – the supermarkets and so on – will take only perfect-looking specimens, which means that the remaining lightly blemished or not quite evenly formed items are sold for a song, even though they taste every bit as good as their idealized brethren.

Townies have no ready access to farm shops, but their special bonus is the wealth of small shops catering to specific local communities. Asian stores can provide ripe pickings in the form of big bunches of fresh herbs, as well as spices in cheap plastic packaging, which can be decanted into airtight containers back home. Don't be tempted to buy huge quantities of ground spices, however, unless you use them on an epic scale, as they will lose their power swiftly. Whole spices, on the other hand, are quite a different matter, and have a long shelf-life that makes them worth buying in some quantity. Other choice treasures to be found in Asian shops include vegetables, poppadums, tamarind and so on. Greek Cypriot groceries also yield good-value herbs, vegetables and fruit, as well as excellent dairy produce, olives and other pickled vegetables. Middle Eastern shops have more of the same, and look out for nuts and dried fruits of superb quality and value. Caribbean cornershops can come up trumps on herbs, but it is the fruit that is particularly appealing, with exotics such as mangoes going for a healthy price.

Herbs
A handful of fresh herbs can make an enormous difference to a simple dish, lifting it straight out of the ordinary – think of a few leaves of basil scattered over a tomato salad, for instance. Unfortunately, the small plastic packs of herbs sold

in supermarkets are very expensive, and contain either far more than you need for any one recipe or not nearly enough. The answer is to grow herbs yourself, or at least make a point of growing those that you use most. You don't need to be particularly green-fingered to grow herbs, nor do you need a vast garden. Actually, you don't need a garden at all. A windowbox will do, or a few capacious containers by the kitchen door. An initial investment in plants bought from a garden centre (which, incidentally will cost little more than a packet or two of cut herbs, but can yield far more over a season) and compost will pay you back royally. Within a matter of weeks, you will be able to pick exactly the right quantity of herbs for the dish you are cooking, with no waste, and increased quotas of flavour and satisfaction.

Adaptable planning

Adaptable planning is what you should aim for when you are determined to drum up impressively good food on next to nothing. Another way of putting it is that old saying, 'Waste not, want not'. Irritating it may be, but there is some truth in it. Thrift is a bit of an old-fashioned virtue but it is not the same as penny-pinching. Making the most of what's on offer just makes sense.

Let us suppose that you start with a chicken. Well, the flesh on one small bird may only be enough to feed four people, but then there is the carcass. From that you can make stock, and if you remember to soak some dried beans or split peas overnight you can cook up a superb, filling, thick soup the next day which, along with bread, cheese and some fruit, will be enough to satisfy anyone. Now, if you poach the chicken instead of, say, roasting it, you would have the stock ready made in the form of the poaching liquid, and the flesh will be delightfully moist, perfect for cold eating, shredded in salads or in big hearty sandwiches, and possibly enough for both. Or you could eat some of it hot, with a simple dipping sauce made of soy sauce, ginger, spring onions and lime juice.

Never waste anything if it can be helped. Stale bread has 101 uses, from croutons for soup, or pedestrian but very useful breadcrumbs (which can be stored in the freezer), to fashionable crostini – grill and rub with garlic, then maybe rub a halved tomato over them, drizzle with olive oil, season lightly and eat on their own or with drinks, soups, salads and so on. Too much milk, in danger of going off? Make rice pudding or a light junket, or cook up a white sauce, simmering it slowly to improve the flavour, which can be used to dress up foods, or for a vegetable gratin, or even as the basis of a soufflé – it freezes well, if you have a freezer. Slightly sour milk can be used to make soda bread, or yeast-risen bread. I could go on, but I won't. I reckon you've got the gist by now.

Plan meals roughly but be prepared to overhaul your plan as you shop. Revise the whole caboodle if you spot something that is totally irresistible for a good price.

Careful planning also means that you can afford to use some of the more fashionable and expensive items that are now so readily available. In the menu on page 39, the centrepiece is pizza with rocket leaves and mascarpone, both pricy items. Since most of the other ingredients are relatively cheap in season you can still balance the books, and have your starter, pizza and pudding and eat them.

The recipes

The recipes in this book are grouped together in menus, usually for two or four people. With the exception of the Harvest Feast and the East-meets-West Birthday Banquet (both of which feed more than four) each menu costs no more than a fiver to cook in total. Of course, this magic £5 barrier can easily be broken if you shop at expensive stores and without any great attention to detail. So all I can say is that it really is possible to bring the menus in at the right price if you are prepared to work at it.

Throughout the past year I have put together a list of well over 500 prices, gathered throughout the seasons from a wide selection of sources, and recipe costings have been based on these. I have calculated the cost of a teaspoon of this and a tablespoon of that, 30 g of one thing and 100 g of another, sticking with the relevant seasonal price (a strawberry in late June is far cheaper than an imported strawberry in mid-winter).

Friends have objected that if you buy a whole packet of, say, polenta for the pudding on page 76, you will be laying out considerably more dosh than the proportion allowed for in my costings. True, but if you are sensible you won't let the rest go to waste, so I don't see that this makes my method of calculating prices untenable. Necessity is the mother of invention, they say, and it is amazing what can be conjured up with half a packet of this and a little bit of that. It all comes back to 'Waste not, want not'. Occasionally I've harnessed two menus together to show what can be done with leftovers and the byproducts of cooking – the Two-times-two menus on pages 149–156 are good examples.

Every last ingredient in each recipe has been taken into consideration, including a few pence for seasonings. There is no reason why you should stick rigidly to whole menus. However, if you do mix and match recipes to suit you I cannot guarantee that you will be able to conjure up a whole meal for that sacred fiver, but even so it shouldn't break the bank.

Cook's notes

Before you start to cook from this book, take a minute or so to read these notes, which gather together the basic conventions that I adhere to when I write recipes.

All spoon measurements are rounded. I use a standard 5 ml teaspoon and 15 ml tablespoon. Eggs are large, and free range if possible (yes, even on a fiver, but you'll have to buy them from a farm shop, which may be an impossibility for town-dwellers). All herbs are fresh, unless otherwise stated, with the exception of bay leaves, which are just as good dried as fresh. I always use extra virgin olive oil, both for cooking and in dressings, since nowadays the cheaper supermarket brands are within the price range of most people and are not at all bad. However, if you are not partial to the taste of extra virgin olive oil, buy what is simply labelled 'olive oil', which has a lighter flavour. Pepper has to be freshly ground or it is not worth using. Likewise, nutmeg must be freshly grated.

I have assumed that you will stick with either the metric or the Imperial measurements, whichever you feel most comfortable with. In most cases a bit of swapping will cause no great disasters – after all, the good cook always tastes and adjusts as she or he cooks – but with cakes and other items that require precise ratios of ingredients it could make a radical difference. Better safe than sorry. Which brings me straight to the final point. Except for cakes and the like, recipes should never be regarded as a set of rules carved in stone. They are guidelines only. I cannot gauge the exact strength of the chillies you will use, or the exact diameter of your saucepan, or the heat emitted by your gas rings or electric burners, or how finely you will chop finely chopped herbs. There are so many variables that every cook must take responsibility for what they are cooking, making minor adjustments as necessary.

SUMMER

Sojourn in *Cosmopolitan* Wye

I used to think that Wye was just like any other small rural town, except that it happened to have an agricultural college in it, and I only knew that because one of my school friends went there. When I finally got around to visiting the place I was charmed, but not surprised, by the winding main street with its quaint old houses oozing character. This is Kent, after all, Garden of England and all that ... it's what one would expect.

The surprises started piling in when I met our hosts, Harriet Festing and Kumar Vasanthakumar, and their two deliciously dark-eyed daughters, Molly and Daisy. This small family sums up the unexpected side of Wye. Here, in quaint rural Kent, is a melting pot of people of all nationalities. Some come to study at the college for a few years, then return to their native countries, while others like Kumar, originally from Sri Lanka, stay on, settling down to throw their own special qualities and culture into the pot.

Every week a van arrives, toting spices and exotica to the international community. An enormous bonus to keen cooks and one that I wish I had access to where I live. Kumar can buy not only lemon grass and ginger but also rarer herbs such as curry leaves and *rampe* (pandanus leaf), which bring a true flavour of Sri Lanka to his cooking. Just outside the town, more ex-students have set up a thriving organic market gardening business at Ripple Farm, distributing what they grow through an organic box scheme. Anyone who joins the scheme pays £5 a week for a magnificent box filled to the brim with freshly picked organic produce. A scenic stroll across fields takes Harriet to Perry Court Pick-Your-Own Farm, and when time is too short for a spell out in the fields, the farm-shop prices and the quality of the produce put the local supermarkets to shame. All in all, an idyllic, tailor-made place for feasting for a fiver.

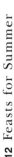

1

A spicy *supper* for four

La Daube Dizef

Kumar's Beetroot Curry

Sri Lankan Cucumber Sambal

Kumar and I joined forces to cook supper together, a spicy affair to be eaten sitting on the ground in the Sri Lankan way, which is how the family shares meals together all the time. The night was so warm and balmy, with just a gentle breeze, that we took the mats outside and ate on the lawn by candlelight. Kumar talked of his life in Sri Lanka and we all swapped family histories late into the night, long after we had eaten our fill of this unexpectedly felicitous blend of spice-laden dishes from one large island off the coast of India and another off the coast of Africa.

La Daube Dizef

This spicy dish of eggs in a hot tomato sauce is something I came across in Mauritius, and is characteristic of the island's multicultural make-up. The name itself is a corruption of the French *daube des oeufs*, stew of eggs, which it transforms into something exotic and exciting without breaking the bank. Serve it simply with rice or puffy, tender naan bread, or do as we did and serve it as part of a selection of spicy dishes.

6 eggs, hard-boiled and shelled
2–4 tablespoons sunflower or vegetable oil
450 g (1 lb) new potatoes, boiled in their skins until tender, halved or quartered if large
2 onions, sliced
4 garlic cloves, crushed
2 small chillies, deseeded and sliced
2.5 cm (1 inch) fresh root ginger, grated
1 tablespoon chopped parsley
leaves from 2 sprigs of thyme
225 g (8 oz) tomatoes, skinned and roughly chopped
a pinch of sugar
½ tablespoon tomato purée
125 ml (4 fl oz) water
400 g (14 oz) tin of petits pois, drained
4 tablespoons roughly chopped coriander
salt

Fry the eggs in 2 tablespoons of the oil over a lively heat until browned on all sides. Drain on kitchen paper. Brown the new potatoes in the same oil and put them to drain with the eggs.

In the same oil, adding more if necessary, fry the onions until lightly browned. Throw in the garlic, chillies, ginger, parsley and thyme. Stir for a couple of minutes, then add the tomatoes. Let the mixture cook and reduce down for 5 minutes, stirring once or twice, then add the sugar, tomato purée, salt and water. Bring up to the boil, simmer for a couple of minutes, then return the eggs and potatoes to the pan. Stir in the petits pois and let the whole lot simmer for a few more minutes to heat through properly. Taste and adjust the seasonings, then stir in the coriander. Serve with rice.

Kumar's Beetroot Curry

Kumar and I share a passion for beetroot – as long as it is not soaked in rough vinegar, which spoils its wonderful, sweet, earthy flavour in one fell swoop. This dish came as quite a revelation to me. It is a subtle, aromatic curry made with coconut milk, which brings out all that is best in beetroot, not least the stunning colour. The beetroot goes in raw, cut into strips, and cooks remarkably quickly, but retains a hint of crispness that is lost when it is cooked whole. Kumar adds a few fresh curry leaves and a small section of *rampe*, which is what I would call pandanus leaf. Although both of these are available from specialist shops I was unable to get hold of them when I cooked this curry at home, yet it still tasted superb.

about 450g (1 lb) raw beetroot
2 onions, chopped
2 tablespoons sunflower or vegetable oil
1 teaspoon cumin seeds
a pinch of fenugreek seeds
¼ teaspoon brown mustard seeds
7.5 cm (3 inch) length of pandanus leaf, cut into slivers (optional)
8 curry leaves (optional)
3–4 green chillies, quartered lengthways and deseeded
300 ml (½ pint) fresh coconut milk (see page 18)
salt

Peel the beetroot and slice them about as thick as a £1 coin. Cut the slices into strips about 1 cm (½ inch) wide. Fry the onions in the oil in a wide frying pan for about 3 minutes, then add the spices, pandanus leaf and curry leaves if using, green chillies and salt. When the mustard seeds start to jump, add the beetroot and cook for 5 minutes on a medium heat. Add the coconut milk, cover and simmer gently for 10 minutes, then uncover and cook for a further 15 minutes or so, until the beetroot is tender.

Sri Lankan Cucumber Sambal

Kumar made us a typical Sri Lankan sambal, a side dish lodged somewhere between a salad and a relish. He uses another special Sri Lankan ingredient, Maldive fish, which is actually boiled, smoked and dried bonito – the Sri Lankan equivalent of the shrimp pastes and fish sauces used in South-east Asian cooking. Sadly it is not readily available in my patch of Northamptonshire so I used anchovy paste instead (actually Gentleman's Relish, but the anchovy purée that you get in tubes, or anchovy essence, would give much the same flavour).

1 cucumber, peeled
2 teaspoons pounded Maldive fish, or ½ tablespoon anchovy paste, purée or essence
1 red onion, halved and sliced
3–4 tablespoons thick coconut milk (see page 19)
juice of 1 lime
salt

Cut the cucumber in half lengthways, then slice it thinly. Soak in salted water for 10 minutes, then drain and squeeze out excess moisture with your hands. Add the cucumber to the rest of the ingredients and mix together thoroughly.

A seaside *lunch* for four

Battered Plaice and **Herb Sandwich**

Griddled Potato, Tomato and **Red Onion Salad**

We all piled into the car, my two little sprogs, Florence and Sidney, their nanny, Jennine, and yours truly, and headed off for a day at the seaside. The pebbly beach at Whitstable entranced the small ones, keeping them busy with marine life exploration (the transparent jellyfish marooned well away from the water proved particularly fascinating) while I was sidetracked by the oyster museum and the sparklingly fresh fish to be had on the harbourside. The small plaice that had been brought in that morning sparkled with freshness, their orange spots verging on fluorescent. They were just within our budget, and soon we were bowling back to Wye with a wonderful haul stashed in the boot. Luckily, Jennine and I managed to persuade Flo and Sid that the jellyfish was best left on the beach ...

Battered Plaice and Herb Sandwich

If you can get good fresh plaice at a reasonable price, this is an excellent way to make four small fish or two larger ones stretch to feed a hungry foursome. Ask your fishmonger to fillet them for you, and save the bones to make stock. Since many people lack access to a good fishmonger, I'll admit that this also works well with frozen plaice fillets, injecting vigour and life into what can be a dull fish.

Use whatever tender-leaved herbs you can lay your hands on, taking parsley as the base. Sharp-flavoured sorrel is particularly good with deep-fried fish, acting rather like a squeeze of lemon juice or vinegar, but unless you grow it yourself it can be rather expensive. Incidentally, if you do have room to grow plants, then sorrel is a gem – it thrives in the garden, or in a container, and increases in quantity year after year. Lovely in soups and to make sauces for fish.

4 small or 2 large plaice, filleted

sunflower or vegetable oil for frying

flour for dusting

salt and pepper

For the batter

225g (8 oz) plain flour

½ teaspoon salt

1 egg, separated

1 tablespoon sunflower oil

300 ml (½ pint) lager

125 ml (4 fl oz) water

For the herb filling

45g (1½ oz) mixed tender-leaved herbs – parsley, sorrel, mint, chives, etc

15g (½ oz) soft breadcrumbs

2 garlic cloves, roughly chopped

4 tablespoons olive oil

a dash of lemon juice, if no sorrel is used

To prepare the batter, sift the flour with the salt, make a well in the centre and add the egg yolk, oil and half the lager. Mix, gradually drawing in the flour to make a smooth batter, adding more lager as you go until it is all incorporated. Whisk in the water. Let the batter stand for half an hour if you have the time. Literally just before using, whisk the egg white until it forms soft peaks and fold it into the batter.

To make the herb filling, put all the ingredients into a food processor and process to a mush. Set aside a generous tablespoonful for the Griddled Potato, Tomato and Red Onion Salad (see below). Heat about 1 cm (½ inch) of oil in a wide frying pan until there is a gentle heat haze – about 185°C/360°F or when a cube of bread fizzles instantly and excitedly as soon as it enters the oil and begins to brown within 10–20 seconds. Meanwhile, dry the plaice fillets on each side with kitchen paper and season with salt and pepper, then sandwich them together in pairs, skin-side out, with a thick smear of the herb filling in the middle. Dust lightly with flour on each side, then dip them into the batter one by one, coating evenly, and lay them in the oil. Cook for about 1–2 minutes on

each side, then drain briefly on kitchen paper. Season with a little extra salt. Serve quickly while still hot and crisp.

Griddled Potato, Tomato and Red Onion Salad

I created this salad specially to accompany the plaice and herb sandwiches, sharing both the herb mixture and some of the oil. If you wanted to cook it separately, as well you might since it is very good indeed, add a tablespoon of chopped mixed parsley, chives and mint and replace the hot oil with 2–3 tablespoons of sunflower or olive oil.

2 red (or white) onions, thinly sliced

2 teaspoons salt

1½ tablespoons white wine vinegar

1 tablespoon caster sugar

650g (1½ lb) main-crop but slightly waxy potatoes (e.g. Estima or Cara), boiled in their skins until just done but no more

a little oil for brushing

450g (1 lb) tomatoes, cut into rough chunks

1 tablespoon herb mixture from the plaice

3 tablespoons hot oil from cooking the plaice

pepper

Begin by mixing the sliced onions with the salt, vinegar and sugar. Leave for ½–1 hour, stirring occasionally, then squeeze the now floppy onions with your hands and place in a salad bowl. Reserve their juices.

Peel the cooked potatoes and slice them about 1 cm (½ inch) thick. Pre-heat a ridged griddle thoroughly, then brush lightly with a little oil. Brush each side of each potato slice with oil and griddle until striped with dark marks on either side. Alternatively they can be grilled or barbecued. Add to the onions, together with the tomatoes, the herb mixture and the juice from the onions. Mix and season with pepper, but no more salt. Just before serving, mix in the hot oil from cooking the fish.

menu

3

A family *picnic* for four to six

Tortilla

Kumar's Sri Lankan Carrot Salad

Summer Pudding

Take the winding road south out of Wye and it snakes you steeply up to the brow of an escarpment. After a mile or two the view beckons you to pull over and stop. From the top you can see right across England, or so it seems when the weather is clear. A wooden sign points the way over the windswept fields to the Devil's Kneading Trough. In this wide hollow in the hill we spread out our rugs and opened the hamper. The children hurtled from one end to another, hair streaming out behind them, working up a good appetite for the picnic food we had brought with us. This was no sandwiches and pop affair but a coming together of Eastern and Western portable foods.

Tortilla

Tortilla is one of the great dishes of Europe, incredibly simple and outstandingly good. The thickest of all the omelettes, it consists of just a handful of cheap ingredients – eggs, potatoes and onions are the main ones – transformed into one of the best cold foods by virtue of the powers of extra virgin olive oil and clever technique. You can make a form of tortilla more quickly and cheaply than the method I give here but it will never taste as good. Taking the time to stew the potatoes slowly in the olive oil is the only way to achieve the sublime taste of a classic Spanish tortilla.

If you want a change, you can add other ingredients – peppers, perhaps, or slices of ham or chorizo – but don't be tempted to use tortilla as a dustbin dish for leftovers. When it comes down to it, the plain potato and onion version remains the best of all.

Enjoy tortilla as the centrepiece of a cold lunch or a picnic, or serve it in smaller portions, as they do in Spain, with pre-prandial drinks, or even as a starter. Though it can be eaten hot or warm, it tastes best at room temperature.

olive oil
3 medium-sized potatoes (main-crop but not too floury), peeled and thinly sliced
1 onion, thinly sliced
sunflower oil
8 eggs, lightly beaten
2 garlic cloves, crushed
salt and pepper

Pour a thin layer of olive oil into a wide, heavy-based frying pan. Pile in all the potatoes and onion, then pour over enough oil (I use a mixture of olive and sunflower) to just about cover. Cover with a lid and stew very gently until the vegetables are tender. Allow at least half an hour. The potatoes and onion should be meltingly soft but not brown. Lift out with a slotted spoon and drain on kitchen paper. Beat the eggs with the garlic and plenty of salt and pepper. Add the warm potatoes and onion, then set aside for some 15–30 minutes before continuing.

Pre-heat the grill. Heat 3 tablespoons of the oil used for stewing the potatoes in a 23–30 cm (9–12 inch) frying pan over a medium heat. Tip in the egg and potato mixture and smooth it down. Cook until three-quarters set. The sides should be a rich brown when eased away from the pan. Finish by browning under the grill. Check that the tortilla is just set through but still moist. Cool for a few minutes in the pan, then turn out. Serve at room temperature, in wedges.

Kumar's Sri Lankan Carrot Salad

The method used for cooking this dish of curried carrots is very similar to that used for Kumar's Beetroot Curry on page 14 but the results are surprisingly different. Though the aromatic carrots are also superb hot, Kumar often serves them cold as a salad.

1 large onion, chopped
2 tablespoons sunflower oil
¼ teaspoon black mustard seeds
½ teaspoon cumin seeds
a pinch of fenugreek seeds
a handful of curry leaves (optional)
a small piece of pandanus leaf (optional – see page 14)
2–3 green chillies, quartered lengthways and deseeded
450g (1 lb) carrots, cut into batons 5 cm (2 inches) long
½ teaspoon ground turmeric
300ml (½ pint) coconut milk (see below)
salt

Fry the onion in the oil for about 3 minutes, then add the mustard, cumin and fenugreek seeds, the curry leaves and pandanus leaf if using, green chillies and salt and continue cooking until the onion is golden. Add the carrots and turmeric and cook for further 3–4 minutes on a medium heat, stirring frequently.

Add the coconut milk, bring to the boil and simmer, covered, for 10 minutes or until the carrots are tender. Taste and adjust the seasoning, then serve hot, warm or cold.

Making coconut milk

The cheapest way to make coconut milk is also, very conveniently, the best – from fresh coconut. Tinned coconut milk works out about three times more costly and although it is a useful standby it has an unpleasant, slimy texture when boiled down. If you can't lay your hands on a fresh coconut (many supermarkets stock them now but, failing that, West Indian and Asian food stores are the best sources ... oh, and the fairground, but that's a bit hit and miss), you can try using desiccated coconut, or diluting some of the hard creamed coconut that comes in small, waxy blocks. Once made up, coconut milk can be stored in the fridge for up to 48 hours.

1 *Using fresh coconut*
First you must breach the tough walls of the coconut. It helps if you have a second pair of

hands to steady the coconut but it's not impossible without. Pierce the coconut through two of the three 'eyes' using a drill, a bradawl, or a strong skewer and a meat mallet. Drain out the coconut juice but don't waste it. Chilled, it makes a very refreshing drink. Grab hold of a hammer and tap the coconut firmly all over to loosen the flesh inside. Now, holding the coconut on its side, repeatedly bash it heavily at the centre of the 'ribs' that run from top to bottom until it cracks in half (be determined – it will split in the end if you persevere). Alternatively, head outside and hurl the coconut down onto a hard paved or concrete area so that it shatters. Rinse thoroughly, and dry before continuing.

Kumar has a very nifty hand-turned machine which neatly grates the white flesh out of the shell, but assuming you are not so well equipped, ease out the flesh in large chunks, then grate them by hand. Put the coconut flesh into a bowl and pour over 600 ml (1 pint) hot water. Leave for a few minutes, then strain, squeezing out the milk with your hands. This is thick coconut milk, which is what is called for in the cucumber sambal on page 14.

Return the debris to the bowl and repeat the squeezing and straining once more to produce thin coconut milk. Mix thin and thick together and you have medium coconut milk, which is what you will need for most recipes.

2 *Using desiccated coconut:*
When you are out shopping, make sure that you do not pick up sweetened desiccated coconut by mistake. Put 250 g (9 oz) unsweetened desiccated coconut into a food processor and add 300 ml (½ pint) hot water. Process briefly, then tip into a sieve and strain off the milk, squeezing it out with your hands, to give thick coconut milk. Repeat once more for thin milk. Mix the two together for medium milk.

3 *Using creamed coconut:*
Grated or finely chopped creamed coconut can be stirred straight into the cooking liquid in the pan or it can be diluted in hot water to the desired consistency.

Summer Pudding

This has to be one of my all-time top-ten puddings. When the sun is shining, head off to that pick-your-own farm and get picking, so that you can enjoy summer pudding made with the freshest, juiciest fruit imaginable. One small note – use a decent loaf of bread. Sliced white may be very convenient but when soaked with juice it turns unpleasantly slimy – a horribly cruel demise for one of the great British puddings.

I like to use crème de cassis, the French blackcurrant liqueur, to add depth of flavour to the juices but if you don't have any, try adding a splash of undiluted Ribena or other blackcurrant cordial. If you take your pudding on a picnic, don't forget to take a sturdy shallow plate as well to turn it out on – cardboard disposables won't do.

750g (1 lb 10 oz) mixed summer fruit – raspberries, red, white and blackcurrants, tayberries, loganberries, blackberries, cherries, blueberries, etc
150g (5 oz) caster sugar
2 tablespoons crème de cassis or Ribena
1 medium loaf of good-quality white bread, thinly sliced, crusts removed

Mix the fruit with the sugar in a saucepan. If you have time, cover with a tea towel or clingfilm and leave for a few hours to get the juices running. Place the pan over the heat and bring gently up to the boil, then simmer for about 3 minutes. Draw off the heat and stir in the cassis or Ribena. Carefully spoon out about 2 tablespoons of juice and set aside in a small bowl.

Rinse a 1 litre (1¾ pint) bowl out with cold water, then shake out the excess. Cut a round out of one piece of bread to fit the bottom of the bowl, then cut the remaining slices into more or less triangular wedges. Line the sides of the bowl with wedges of bread, nudging them tightly together so that there are no gaps. Spoon in all the fruit and their juices (apart from the reserved juice). Cover the surface with more wedges of bread. Find a saucer that fits neatly inside the bowl, place it on the upper layer of bread, then weight it down with weights, bags of rice, tins of baked beans, or whatever comes to hand. Leave in the fridge overnight.

Remove the weights and saucer, run a thin-bladed knife around the edges of the pudding, then invert it on to a shallow serving plate. Brush the reserved juices over any blotchy, whitish patches and then just pour the last few drops over the pudding to burnish it. Serve with cream, if the budget allows.

Many of Kumar and Harriet's friends are students at the college, and one of the things they love aboout going round to visit them in their halls of residence is the food, as multinational as the students themselves. When Kenneth, a Kenyan post-graduate, invited us round to lunch, we accepted with alacrity. Like all students, Kenneth has to budget carefully to make his meagre funds stretch, so I suggested that we took a contribution to his meal. Luckily, the rice salad went surprisingly well with the rich and unusual chicken dish he cooked for us in the small kitchen he shares with four other students.

menu

4

A student *lunch* for four

Kenneth's Chicken Abigail

Rice Salad with **Apricots**

Kenneth's Chicken Abigail

I have to admit that I was a little taken aback when I saw Kenneth slipping processed cheese slices into the saucepan. The result, however, is astonishingly delicious. His cooking method is unorthodox, or so it seemed to me, but this, he tells me, is how his Grandmother Abigail used to cook chicken and he sees no reason to deviate. Except for the cheese slices, that is ...

4 chicken thighs, cut in half, or 1 small chicken, cut into 4 portions
1 onion, chopped
110 g (4 oz) mushrooms, sliced
1 tablespoon sunflower oil
2 tomatoes, skinned, deseeded and roughly chopped
4 processed cheese slices
300 ml (½ pint) coconut milk (see page 18) or ordinary milk
salt and pepper

Put the chicken pieces into a pan with the onion and enough water to come about two-thirds of the way up the chicken. Season with salt and pepper. Bring up to the boil and simmer, turning the meat occasionally, until the water has reduced down to a very thin layer on the bottom of the pan. Now add the mushrooms and oil and cook for a further 10 minutes or so, allowing the chicken and mushrooms to brown slightly. Next add the tomatoes and cook until they have collapsed down to a mush. Finally add the cheese slices, stir, and then pour in the milk. Bring up to the boil and simmer for a final 10 minutes, until the chicken is cooked through.

Rice Salad with Apricots

Kumar had cooked us a huge vat of rice to eat with our supper and there was oodles left over. It seemed a shame to waste it, so instead I dressed it up to make a lively rice salad to take to lunch with the students. When I wrote out the recipe later on, I realized that the salad would have tasted even better if I had started on it as soon as the rice was cooked, so that the hot rice could absorb some of the dressing as it cooled. Either way, it tastes good, and is just the thing for a summer lunch or a barbecue. It also goes very well with Kenneth's Chicken Abigail.

about 340 g (12 oz) long grain rice, cooked and drained
1 small onion, finely chopped
1 garlic clove, finely chopped
1 tablespoon sunflower or olive oil
6 spring onions, thinly sliced
85 g (3 oz) ready-to-eat dried apricots, finely diced
2–3 tablespoons chopped coriander

For the dressing
1½ tablespoons white wine vinegar
½ teaspoon Dijon mustard
4 tablespoons sunflower or olive oil
plenty of salt and freshly ground pepper

As soon as the rice is cooked, tip it into a sieve and rinse with hot water, then leave to drain again. Make the dressing while the rice is still hot by whisking the vinegar with the mustard, salt and pepper, then gradually whisking in the oil. Taste and adjust the seasoning, bearing in mind that it needs to be slightly sharper and saltier than usual to balance the blandness of the rice. Tip the rice and dressing into a bowl and mix, then leave to cool – refrigerate if leaving overnight.

To finish the salad, fry the onion and garlic gently in the oil until tender and translucent. Mix into the rice along with the remaining ingredients. Taste again and adjust the seasoning one final time.

Late *Summer* in Barnstaple

In time-honoured fashion the children were getting unbearably fractious – well, weren't we all? – by the time we turned off the main road. That constant refrain of 'Will we be there soon?' had risen to fever pitch, but at last the answer was truthfully, 'Yes!' It was the week before the August Bank Holiday and, like so many others, we were motoring down to spend a week at the seaside, in one of Devon's prettiest little backwaters. As Appledore opened up before us the tension evaporated like magic. What a glorious sight!

The small town stretched out in front of us along the banks of the Taw estuary, seagulls wheeling and diving over the tidal waters. Along the quay strolled holidaymakers, licking ice-creams and armed with shrimping nets, with the bulk of the town looking on approvingly. It seemed unspoilt – no frenetic amusement arcades, no neon signs or blaring music – a charming throwback to the simplicity of the Fifties and early Sixties. And the light, with its luminous Mediterranean clarity ... no wonder this has become something of a haven for artists.

We were here, in fact, at the suggestion of one such artist, Dawn Frost, having discovered a slightly tenuous family connection. Her house is right on the estuary, with blissful views over the rise and fall of the tide. Lucky woman, and lucky us, being able to share the view for a few days from our own rented cottage at the other end of town.

August is the season of glut and plenty, and the small butcher's-come-greengrocer's on the New Quay was overflowing with local bounty. Runner beans in big heaps, the last of the broad beans, blushing plums, apricots and scarlet tomatoes outside, and home-cooked meats and hog's puddings, a traditional local sausage, on the inside. A few yards further on, another shop sold buckets and spades, crabbing lines and ice-creams, again locally made and of rather fine quality. Both stock the famous, irresistible Devon clotted cream. The fishermen bring in their haul in the early morning and much of it makes its way up to Barnstaple, to the little fish shop outside the marvellous pannier market, which was where Dawn led me bright and early one morning.

There has been a pannier market in the centre of Barnstaple for hundreds of years – a tradition that I envy enormously. I wish fervently that I had a market like this on my doorstep. Indeed, every town, small or large, should have one, or something like it. The name gives you some idea of the scope of it. In the past, and even now to some extent, local market gardeners, farmers and smallholders would load up their panniers or baskets, many would sling them over the back of their horse, bicycle or, eventually, jalopy, and set off to town to rendezvous with their colleagues for a morning of selling and socializing. To this day, people who grow produce on a small scale, within 10 miles of the town, are offered a very low rate for a place in the market. Many just set up a small folding table with their wares laid out upon it. The result is a hall packed full of truly seasonal produce, most of it phenomenally fresh, picked, plucked and gathered within a matter of hours, and all of it selling at heart-warmingly reasonable prices. Some women sell pasties, Devon splits and other baked goods, while one of my favourite stands was that of an elderly lady with a couple of baskets of gnarled apples. The varieties were rare, coming from two old trees that grew in her garden. One was a small, gold and red eating apple with that marvellous sharp, rich, sweet flavour that lingers

5

Supper for two on the balcony

Peppers Sorrento

Mussels with Tomato, Basil and **Garlic,** with **Shoestring Chips** and **Garlic Mayonnaise**

Previous double page (Clockwise from left): Peppers Sorrento; Mussels with Tomato, Basil and Garlic, with Shoestring Chips and Garlic Mayonnaise

only for a day or two after picking, the other an early cooker, which I later discovered baked to a light, golden fluff.

There were oceans of runner beans – but about the best that you are likely to come across – lots of tomatoes, local farm cheeses, free range eggs aplenty, bunches of aromatic herbs, more plums and even, at the WI stall, some of the incredibly fashionable Italian *cavolo nero*, or black cabbage. One farmer sold clotted cream, and had a big tin basin of it on display, as it used to be before health regulations put paid to such things, the thick crust yellow and enticing above the pure, creamy white interior. The cream that was for selling came, quite properly, in sealed tubs. And for the sweet-toothed, a seductive shop at the end of the market sent out heavenly wafts of sugary enticement as the staff stirred vats of molten fudge. Not to be missed, in my estimation. Outside the main market is the original 'butcher's row', a collection of butcher's shops competing one with the other and providing the best of local beef, pork, lamb and poultry. This is what shopping should be all about, drawing inspiration and inestimable pleasure from the choice of highly seasonal produce. Supermarkets are useful, amenable places but they cannot compete with something like Barnstaple's pannier market.

Dawn and I share a passion for Italy, especially the food, so our brace of menus takes a good deal of inspiration from the Mediterranean, which seems particularly fitting in glorious late-August weather on the shores of the Taw estuary. The menus are inevitably intertwined, sharing, as they do, one base item – home-made mayonnaise – in two very different guises. That's where the similarities end. The first menu was designed to be eaten out on Dawn's balcony, as the last of the light fades away to dark, and distant lights and sounds are all that remain. If you closed your eyes you could almost imagine that you were, perhaps, in Sorrento, with

6

A working *lunch* for two

Broad Bean, Oven-dried Tomato and **Bacon Salad**

Seared Chicken and **Peach Sandwich** with **Basil Mayo**

Roast Plums with **Clotted Cream**

the salt scent of the sea in the air and a caressing warm breeze. Even without the idyllic setting, this is an excellent, summery menu, which brings together the flavours of Italy – in the form of tomatoes and perfumed basil, roasted peppers, garlic, anchovies and capers – with a dash of Belgium. Yes, Belgium, and in this case Belgium's most famous and most agreeable culinary discovery – mussels with chips and mayonnaise.

The second menu started out as a simple sandwich sort of a lunch that Dawn and I could share when she took a break from creating one of her mosaic pots. I had leftover mayonnaise and a few leaves of basil, and from these two came the idea for a warm, chunky sandwich, enlivened with the soft fragrance of lightly cooked peaches. Then I discovered that my allowance was not anywhere near spent. So I went foraging and found a haul of broad beans and a few juicy Victoria plums. Suddenly it had turned into an informal three-course luncheon.

Menu 5
Peppers Sorrento

Dawn adores Italy and heads off there as often as she can. Her last trip, with her son, was to Sorrento, just south of Naples. While she was there she gathered, amongst other souvenirs, a bottle of superb locally pressed olive oil and this recipe for roasted peppers with a piquant dressing. One of the things she loves about it is its appearance, with the languid, smoky colours of the peppers and the little amber bubbles of their juice that form in the dressing.

1 red pepper
1 yellow pepper
2 teaspoons capers, rinsed, drained and finely chopped
1 large garlic clove, crushed
about 3 anchovy fillets, finely chopped
2 generous sprigs of oregano, marjoram or parsley, finely chopped
1 generous tablespoon extra virgin olive oil
freshly ground black pepper

Pre-heat the oven to 220°C/425°F/Gas Mark 7.

Roast the peppers whole on a baking tray or in an ovenproof dish for about 20 minutes, until they feel soft and the skins are blistering. Pop straight into a plastic bag and knot it loosely. Leave until cool enough to handle, then pull the skin off the peppers. Quarter, deseed and arrange on either one large plate or 2 individual ones. Save any juices in the bag or that oozed out as the peppers were skinned.

Mix together all the other ingredients in a small bowl, adding fewer or more anchovy fillets depending on how much you like their salty flavour. Add the pepper juices and mix in well. Spoon the dressing over the peppers and then leave until cool. Serve at room temperature or lightly chilled.

Mussels with Tomato, Basil and Garlic

Tender, juicy, plump little mussels are one of life's perfect pleasures (assuming you're not allergic to shellfish), and that is true whatever your budget. Of course, you must buy them from a reputable fishmonger, so you can be sure that they are scrupulously fresh, and you should really cook them the day they are bought. Preparation takes a little time, but is essential to avoid grit and, heaven forbid, the occasional dicey mussel. You can clean the mussels an hour or two in advance, and make the tomatoey base for the juices ahead of time, too. Serve the mussels in wide soup plates, pouring over the juices when the plates are piled high with mussels. Spoons, for scooping up the soupy liquid once the mussels have been eaten, are really the only cutlery you need. However, other essentials are napkins, fingerbowls filled with warm water, and a big bowl in the centre of the table to take the heap of empty shells.

Serves 2 generously as a main course, 4 as a starter

½ onion, chopped
2 tablespoons olive oil
4 garlic cloves, sliced
250g (9 oz) tomatoes, skinned, deseeded and chopped
1 bay leaf
a pinch or two of sugar
1 kg (2¼ lb) mussels
1 glass of white wine (about 125 ml/4 fl oz)
a small handful of basil leaves, roughly shredded
salt and pepper

To make the tomato base, start by frying half the onion in the olive oil until tender. Add the sliced garlic and cook gently, without browning, for 2 minutes. Now add the tomatoes, bay leaf, sugar, pepper and a hint of salt. Turn up the heat and cook fairly swiftly, stirring frequently, until reduced to a very thick sauce (about 5–10 minutes, depending on the width of the pan and the heat). Turn off the heat and leave until needed.

Rinse the mussels, scrape off any barnacles and tear away the tough 'beard' (or, more technically, bissus), which they use to attach themselves to rocks or posts. Discard any mussels that have broken shells, or that stay open even when rapped firmly on the work surface. Rinse again and drain thoroughly.

Put the remaining onion into a pan large enough to hold the mussels with room to spare. Add the white wine and an equal quantity of water and bring up to a rolling boil. Tip in the mussels and clamp the lid on tightly. Shake over a high heat for a few minutes, until the mussels have opened. Discard any that stay firmly closed. Lift the mussels out with a slotted spoon and place in a warm tureen or bowl while you finish the sauce. Quickly strain the cooking juices of the mussels into the tomatoey sauce. Bring up to the boil, stirring to mix, and boil hard for 2 minutes. Taste and adjust the seasoning, then stir in the basil and pour the sauce over the mussels. Serve immediately with the chips and mayonnaise (see page 28). *Bon appétit*.

Shoestring Chips

Chips, mussels and mayo is the great Belgian combination, and boy, do they do it well. If you want to use ready-made oven chips, that's fine, but for a real treat – and a cheap one at that – make them yourself. Be sure to choose a good, floury variety of potato – King Edwards are ideal.

2 large potatoes
oil or other fat for deep-frying
salt

Peel the potatoes and cut into slices about 5 mm (¼ inch) thick. Cut lengthways into batons of the same thickness. Cover with cold water to prevent browning, until you are ready to start the cooking.

Set the oil to heat to 150°C/300°F – or until it bubbles very gently around a cube of bread dropped into it but doesn't brown it. Drain the potatoes thoroughly and pat dry assiduously on kitchen paper or clean tea towels. Deep-fry in 3 batches, allowing them to cook for about 3–4 minutes, without browning, until tender. Drain thoroughly on kitchen paper and leave to cool. Just before eating, reheat the oil, this time to 180°C/350°F. Fry the chips again, in 3 batches, until golden brown.

And now a great tip from my friend Annabel's mum – if you have any brown paper bags, tip the chips into them as soon as they are cooked, then add salt, fold over the top of the bag and shake – the bag absorbs excess fat and the salt gets evenly distributed. Brown paper bags are not so easily found these days, so the alternative is to drain the chips briefly on kitchen paper and then sprinkle with salt. Either way, serve piping hot, with the mussels and mayonnaise, Belgian style.

Mayonnaise

Making mayonnaise in small quantities is a fairly quick affair and it tastes glorious, especially with the sweet mussels and the chips. A dollop of mayo stirred into the juices left in the plate brings an unctuous richness as a final treat. You won't need all the mayonnaise for this meal, so save 2–3 generous tablespoonfuls for another dish, such as the Seared Chicken and Peach Sandwich on page 29.

Serves 3–4

½ garlic clove (optional)
1 egg yolk
½ teaspoon Dijon mustard
1–1½ teaspoons white wine vinegar or tarragon vinegar
60 ml (2 fl oz) olive oil
90 ml (3 fl oz) sunflower oil or other light salad oil
salt and pepper

Put the garlic in a bowl and crush to a paste with a pinch or two of salt. Add the egg yolk and mustard and work together, then mix in 1 teaspoon of the vinegar. Mix the two oils together in a small jug. Whisking constantly, add the oil to the egg yolk mixture a drop at a time. When you get about a third of the way through, you can increase the flow to a slow, steady trickle, but never a stream. When the oil has all been incorporated, taste and adjust the balance of seasonings, adding more vinegar if necessary.

Menu 6
Broad Bean, Oven-dried Tomato and Bacon Salad

This salad is best served warm straight from the pan, so that you can savour the flavours and enjoy the colours at their most vivid. It's worth taking a little trouble over broad beans, especially late in their season. Although the price is often very low, they can be on the large, tough side. It may seem a bit of a chore to skin each individual bean but it pays dividends in terms of taste. Besides, skinning enough beans for a salad for two is not too onerous. Turn on the radio, settle down and enjoy yourself.

650 g (1½ lb) fresh broad beans in their pods, or 175–225 g (6–8 oz) frozen broad beans, thawed
1 thick rasher of streaky bacon, rind removed, cut into narrow strips
1 tablespoon olive or sunflower oil
½ red onion, thinly sliced
1 garlic clove, chopped
1 or 2 oven-dried tomatoes, cut into strips (optional – see below)
½ tablespoon red wine vinegar
½ teaspoon Dijon mustard
¼ teaspoon sugar
salt and pepper

Pod the broad beans if fresh. Blanch in boiling water for 1 minute, then drain. Using a sharp knife, make a slit in the end of each one and pop out the little bright-green beanlet inside. If using frozen broad beans, just let them thaw, then skin in the same way. Finish cooking the beans in fresh water for about 1–2 minutes for frozen, 2–3 minutes for fresh. Drain thoroughly.

Fry the bacon in the oil until lightly browned. Add the beans, onion and garlic and fry for a couple of minutes to heat through and to begin to soften the onion. The idea is that it should retain some of its freshness but have the edge taken off by the heat. Draw off the heat, allow to cool for a minute or so, stir in the oven-dried tomatoes if using, then add the vinegar, mustard, sugar, salt and pepper. Stir to mix evenly and serve hot or warm.

Oven-dried Tomatoes

Oven-dried tomatoes are not the same as sun-dried tomatoes. I like to cook them slowly until they are semi-dried but still slightly fleshy, with intensified flavour and a lightly chewy texture. Here's what you do. Halve the tomatoes across the equator and deseed carefully. Season with salt and leave upside down on a rack to drain for half an hour. Place cut-side up on a tray lined with non-stick baking parchment and bake for about 1½–2 hours at 170°C/325°F/Gas Mark 3. Check regularly towards the end of the cooking time. When they are done they should be rather frizzled round the edges but softly leathery in the centre. If you don't want to use them immediately you can preserve them by packing them into a clean, dry jar, adding a few cloves of garlic if you like, a sprig of thyme or rosemary and maybe a dried chilli or two as well. Add enough oil (olive is best but sunflower is cheaper – you could mix the pair) to cover completely, then store, tightly sealed, in the fridge.

Seared Chicken and Peach Sandwich with Basil Mayo

I've got to admit that I was particularly pleased with this big sandwich. Griddling the peaches brings out their full fragrance, and the warmth of the chicken and the peaches together persuades the basil in the mayonnaise to put on its very best, most aromatic show. Chicken thighs are very cheap, especially if you buy them with the bone in and remove it yourself (just cut down through the flesh along the length of the bone, then use a small, sharp, flexible knife to cut the flesh away from the bone, carefully working your way around it). They also have much more flavour than the more expensive breast meat. Make the most of it!

2 chicken thighs, boned (but not skinned)
juice of ½ lemon
2–3 tablespoons olive oil
1 ciabatta or baguette
1 peach, halved and stoned
a few leaves of Cos lettuce
salt and pepper

For the mayonnaise

a small handful of basil leaves
a pinch of sugar
a pinch of salt
2–3 tablespoons mayonnaise, with or without garlic in it (see page 28)

Marinate the chicken thighs in the lemon juice, olive oil, salt and pepper for at least an hour.

To make the mayonnaise, pound the basil, sugar and salt to a rough paste in a mortar, then work in the mayonnaise (see opposite). Taste and adjust the seasoning.

continued on page 32

continued from page 29

When you are beginning to get peckish, halve the bread lengthways, then wrap it in foil and heat through in a gentle oven. Oil the griddle pan and set over a strong heat (or heat up the grill and line the grill pan with foil). Leave to heat up for 3 or 4 minutes at least. Shake excess marinade off the chicken and lay it on the griddle (or under the grill, close to the heat at first). Leave undisturbed for 3 minutes and don't worry about the smoke. Turn and repeat on the other side. Meanwhile, brush the peach with oil and lay it on the griddle. Leave for about 3 minutes, then turn and leave for another 3 minutes. Reduce the heat under the griddle so that the chicken can cook through without burning to smithereens – it'll need another 3 or 4 minutes or so, turning it once or twice.

When chicken and peaches are nearly done, start assembling the sandwich. Slather both sides of the inside of the bread with the basil mayonnaise. Line the bottom half with lettuce leaves. As soon as the chicken is done, slice each piece diagonally to form large wedges that are a little easier to eat. Slice the peaches roughly, too, then load the bread with chicken and peach. Clamp on the top, cut in half and tuck in.

Previous page
(Clockwise from top left):
Broad Bean, Oven-dried
Tomato and Bacon Salad;
Seared Chicken and
Peach Sandwich with Basil
Mayo; Roast Plums with
Clotted Cream

Roast Plums with Clotted Cream

Here is another idea that I've picked up from my chum Annabel for a simple but extremely good pudding that is a doddle to make. The plums are roasted in a buttered dish with sugar until tender and caramelized. Add a dash of clotted cream and you are in seventh heaven. And if you can't get hold of clotted cream at a reasonable cost, then a dab or two of crème fraîche or just ordinary cream will do the trick.

10–15 g (⅓–½ oz) butter
3–4 plums (Victorias are ideal), halved and stoned
30 g (1 oz) light muscovado sugar
clotted cream, to serve (optional)

Pre-heat the oven to 200°C/400°F/Gas Mark 6.

Use a little of the butter to grease an ovenproof dish just large enough to hold the plums in a single layer. Arrange the plums in it cut-side up. Sprinkle the sugar over thickly and dot the plums with the last of the butter. Roast for 15–20 minutes, until the plums are tender and the sugar has melted into the juices to form a rosy, rich syrup.

If you wish to brown the plums a little, sprinkle over a touch more sugar and rush under a thoroughly pre-heated grill. Either way, serve hot or warm, with cream.

clotted cre

menu

7

The Marwood *Teas*

Violet Graham's Scones

Margaret Pover's Moist Lemon Cake

Betty Skelly's Chocolate Cake

Betty Skelly's Coffee Cake

Le Progrès au **Chocolat**

A sunny afternoon beckoned, luring us out to explore. 'Let's ring my friend John,' cried Dawn, 'and ask him to drive us up into the hills for tea.' She pointed across the Taw Estuary to the grey-blue hills in the distance. 'The Marwood ladies serve up an amazing tea for a mere £2.50 a head.' So John was called and duly turned up with the beautiful Esmerelda. Esmerelda is his pride and joy, and they've been together now for over 30 years. She is well into her sixties but has lost none of her charm and sparkle, none of her get up and go, none of her power to attract attention and turn heads wherever she goes. A few signs of age are apparent, of course – well, they just don't make them like that anymore – but for an old gal she is remarkably sprightly and youthful. So, with long flowing scarves wrapped round our necks, we expressed our admiration and climbed in. A few seconds to warm up, and then Esmerelda is off, taking us round the bay and up through the meandering, high-hedged lanes that lead to Marwood. I did mention, didn't I, that Esmerelda is a bottle-green vintage Austin?

Right through the summer, the ladies of Marwood put on a sumptuous feast in the village hall at least once a week. It stands only a few yards from the Marwood Gardens and people come from miles around to sample both. The ladies also cater for coach parties and even the odd christening and wedding on request. All profits go to the church, which as you can imagine is spruce and well-kept. For the princely sum of £2.50, each lucky customer gets thinly sliced bread and butter, scones with clotted cream and strawberry jam, and two generous slices of cake, not to mention a sterling brew of tea, served in fine china teacups. Quite a find. The organization is immaculate, with complicated rotas that no one dares stray from. Towards the end of every week the good ladies bake busily, each one producing her own speciality. The formidable Margaret Pover can turn out a mean
continued on page 36

Following page (Clockwise from left): Violet Graham's Scones; Betty Skelly's Chocolate Cake; Margaret Plover's Moist Lemon Cake

Feasts for Summer 33

continued from page 33

lemon cake, Betty Skelly conjures up quick but light chocolate and coffee cakes, while the estimable Violet Graham is a dab hand with the scones, and so on right across the parish.

We're early, so John and Esmerelda drop us off at Mrs Pover's house, while they head off to sort out their own affairs. Mrs P. and I discuss cakes and costs and matters culinary, while Dawn whizzes off to photograph the gardens and the view. Then to tea in the pretty village hall, the tables decked out with checked cloths and brightened with little posies of freshly cut flowers. In the centre is a table laden with a fantastic display of cakes. Tea does, indeed, prove to be a splendid and filling affair, so much so that I beg recipes for a clutch of the best cakes from the Marwood gang before John and Esmerelda return to carry us off home, rattling through the countryside, replete and in high spirits.

Violet Graham's Scones

All the Marwood ladies can turn out a fantastic scone at the drop of a hat but Violet Graham is the acknowledged queen of the light-as-air scone. With such low prices for flour in some supermarkets, she reckons that she could turn out an astonishing 216 scones for a crisp blue fiver. This recipe produces a more manageable batch of around 20 small scones. For a light sheen, brush the tops with a little milk before baking. Serve the scones warm from the oven, with clotted cream and strawberry jam or, failing that, whipped cream or butter and any good jam (the Plum and Walnut Jam on page 48 would be just the ticket).

2 large eggs
milk
450 g (1 lb) self-raising flour
2 teaspoons baking powder
110 g (4 oz) butter, diced
60 g (2 oz) caster sugar

Pre-heat the oven to 220°C/425°F/Gas Mark 7.

Beat the eggs together lightly in a measuring jug, then add enough milk to make up to 300 ml (½ pint) and whisk together lightly. Sift the flour with the baking powder. Rub in the butter until the mixture resembles fine breadcrumbs. Stir in the sugar, then stir in enough of the egg and milk mixture to give a soft but not sticky dough – you may not need it quite all.

Turn out on to a lightly floured work surface and knead lightly. Roll out to a thickness of 1 cm (½ inch) and stamp out 5 cm (2 inch) rounds. Place on greased baking sheets and bake for about 10 minutes, until pale golden brown.

Margaret Pover's Moist Lemon Cake

Mrs Pover, who runs an immaculate bed and breakfast between her bouts of cake-making, reckons that a brace of these lovely, syrupy, sharp lemon cakes will set her back little more than £4. She has been making them all summer long, so she can recite the recipe from memory, and no longer needs to look up quantities. In a matter of minutes she whizzes up a new batch of batter and it's straight into the oven. Her cakes usually get eaten up pretty swiftly, but if needs be they will keep particularly well in an air-tight container in a cool place.

Serves 8

175 g (6 oz) caster sugar
175 g (6 oz) self-raising flour
175 g (6 oz) softened butter
1 level teaspoon baking powder
3 medium eggs
finely grated zest of 1 large lemon
75 ml (2½ fl oz) milk

To finish

3 tablespoons granulated sugar, plus a little extra
juice of 1 large lemon
a few more curls of lemon zest

Pre-heat the oven to 180°C/350°F/Gas Mark 4.

Line the base of a 17.5–20 cm (7–8 inch) cake tin with non-stick baking parchment and grease the sides. Put all the ingredients for the cake into a food processor and process until smooth and evenly mixed, to produce a fairly runny cake batter. Pour into the prepared tin and bake for 40–50 minutes, until a skewer inserted in the centre comes out clean. Let the cake stand in the tin for 5 minutes, then turn out on to a plate. With a fine skewer pierce a dozen or so holes in the cake.

While the cake is in the oven, make the lemon syrup by stirring the 3 tablespoons of sugar into the lemon juice until dissolved. Pour this syrup over the cake once it has been turned out and pierced. Sprinkle the top with a thin, even layer of granulated sugar and then finish with a few extra curls of lemon zest scattered prettily over the top.

Betty Skelly's Chocolate Cake

Betty's cake is another quick and easy one to put together, yielding up a light, plain chocolate sponge of a traditional sort. Last time she totted up the costs she reckoned that it came in at around £1.50 per cake.

She likes to dust the plain butter icing with cocoa to give a dark finish and take the edge off the sweetness. My one suggestion would be to splash out on unrefined icing sugar, with its distinct pale tan colour and mild caramel flavour, which will give the icing an extra dimension.

Serves 8 generously

150 g (5 oz) self-raising flour
30 g (1 oz) cocoa powder
175 g (6 oz) softened butter
175 g (6 oz) caster sugar
3 large eggs

For the butter icing

45 g (1½ oz) softened butter
150 g (5 oz) icing sugar
1 tablespoon cocoa powder, mixed with 2 teaspoons hot water

Pre-heat the oven to 180°C/350°F/Gas Mark 4.

Line the base of a 17.5 cm (7 inch) cake tin with non-stick baking parchment and grease the sides. Sift the flour with the cocoa. Cream the butter and sugar together until light and fluffy. Beat in the eggs one at a time, adding a tablespoonful of flour with the last one. Fold in the remaining flour. Spoon into the cake tin and bake for 35–40 minutes, until a skewer inserted in the centre comes out clean. Leave in the tin for a few minutes, then unmould and leave to cool on a wire rack.

To make the butter icing, cream the butter with the icing sugar and the cocoa mixture until light and fluffy. Spread it over the top of the cake, then use the tines of a fork to make either little tufts and peaks or wavy lines in the icing. Dust lightly with a little extra cocoa powder before serving.

Betty Skelly's Coffee Cake

This is made by the same method as the chocolate cake: just substitute 2 heaped teaspoons of good-quality instant coffee, dissolved in 1 tablespoon of hot water, for the 30 g (1 oz) cocoa powder, adding it with the third egg and the tablespoonful of flour. For the butter icing, replace the cocoa with ½ teaspoon of good-quality instant coffee, dissolved in 1 teaspoon of hot water. Press 10 walnut halves around the edge of the cake to decorate, instead of dusting it with cocoa.

Le Progrès au Chocolat

A grand-sounding name for what is, in effect, a hazelnut and chocolate meringue gâteau. This was my contribution to the Marwood teas the day we visited, though I'm not too sure that the ladies approved of such an indulgent and rich offering. Perhaps they were right, though I'm loath to admit it. It is such a wonderfully over-the-top concoction that maybe it is best saved for a special occasion – a birthday or anniversary, for instance. Despite its grandeur it is very easy to make, and even using good-quality plain chocolate with 70 per cent cocoa solids, which most supermarkets sell these days, it still costs less than a fiver. What's more, it will satisfy eight to ten people quite comfortably.

Make the hazelnut meringue the evening before you intend to serve the Progrès au Chocolat, or at a pinch first thing in the morning, so that you can leave the discs to cool in the oven. This is the best way to avoid unwanted cracks in the surface and, incidentally, works well for baked cheesecakes too.

225 g (8 oz) hazelnuts
340 g (12 oz) caster sugar
30 g (1 oz) cornflour
6 large egg whites
a pinch of salt
¼ teaspoon cream of tartar
1 teaspoon vanilla essence
a little cocoa powder for dusting

For the chocolate cream
200 g (7 oz) good-quality plain chocolate
a small knob of butter
300 ml (½ pint) double cream

Cut out 3 sheets of non-stick baking parchment to line 3 baking sheets. Draw a 20 cm (8 inch) circle on each one, using a plate as a template. Lay the paper, pencil marks downwards, on the baking sheets.

Spread the hazelnuts out on a baking tray and roast in a medium-hot oven for 4–8 minutes, until browned. If they have skins on them, rub them in a tea towel to peel them off. Leave to cool, then grind to a fine powder in a food processor in brief bursts to prevent them becoming pasty. Mix with 225 g (8 oz) of the caster sugar and all of the cornflour.

Pre-heat the oven to 110°C/225°F/Gas Mark ¼. Whisk the egg whites until foamy. Add the salt and cream of tartar and continue whisking until the whites form soft peaks. A spoonful at a time, beat in the remaining sugar until you have stiff, glossy peaks. Whisk in the vanilla essence. Gradually fold in the nut mixture a little at a time with the lightest possible touch, working fast so that the mixture retains as much air as possible.

Using a spatula, spread a third of the mixture over each circle, forming a disc about 1 cm (½ inch) thick. Bake very slowly for 1–1½ hours, until firm and dry to the touch. Carefully lift each meringue and check that the underneath is firm and dry too. If not, cook for another 20 minutes or so until it is done. Don't take the meringues out of the oven but instead, turn off the heat and close the door. Leave to cool completely before taking them out. If time is short you can cool them more quickly on racks but they are far more likely to crack.

To make the chocolate cream, break the chocolate into squares and melt in a bowl set over a pan of gently simmering water (or covered tightly in a microwave at half power, in 1 minute bursts, stirring between bursts). As soon as it has melted, draw it off the heat and beat in the knob of butter. Cool until tepid. Whip the cream and fold it into the chocolate.

Carefully sandwich the 3 hazelnut meringue discs together with the chocolate cream and keep cool or, better still, chill if the weather is sultry and hot. Dust lightly with cocoa just before serving.

8

Midsummer *Italian* menu for two

Pinzimonio

Potato Pizza with **Anchovies, Mascarpone** and **Rocket**

Lemon Mascarpone Ice-cream with **Strawberry Coulis**

This is a menu that costs, according to my final calculation, almost exactly £5 and includes two of the most fashionable, and hence rather pricy, Italian ingredients – rocket and mascarpone. Just because you are on a budget, it doesn't mean that you have to do without the latest luxuries altogether. The first course is a very light form of crudités, i.e. strips of raw vegetables, which will take the edge off your hunger while you wait for the pizzas. The pizzas are filling and unusual in that they do not have a shred of tomato on them but instead are topped with crisply browned slices of potato, mascarpone and oodles of rocket. To balance the healthy lightness of the starter is a fabulous Italian gelato made with mascarpone and lemon juice and smothered in strawberry sauce.

Pinzimonio

Pinzimonio is the pretty name for one of the simplest Italian starters. It also happens to be extremely good, as long as your vegetables are very fresh (this is definitely not an occasion for buying up past-sell-by-date vegetables at a knockdown price). Prepare them no more than an hour or so in advance, and store in sealed plastic bags in the fridge until nearly ready to use.

The 'dip' is a basic DIY affair – each of you makes up his or her own mixture of olive oil, lemon juice, salt and pepper. If you are feeling flush, the lemon juice could be replaced with balsamic vinegar, or you could offer a chilli-infused olive oil (home-made, naturally – just stuff a handful of dried chillies in a bottle and then fill up with olive oil, adding a few cloves of garlic or a sprig or two of thyme and rosemary if you like) as an alternative.

1 carrot, cut into batons
½ fennel bulb, cut into slivers
6 radishes, preferably with their leaves, cleaned
2 celery stalks, cut into batons 10 cm (4 inches) long
60 ml (2 fl oz) extra virgin olive oil
juice of 1 lemon, less the dash used in the strawberry coulis (see page 41)
sea salt and pepper

Shortly before eating, arrange all the vegetables in a basket or bowl lined with a cloth napkin (this is merely for effect, so not absolutely necessary, though it does make a nice touch) and set it on the table. Pour the olive oil and lemon juice into two separate small bowls and place in the centre of the table along with a bowl of sea salt and the pepper mill. Set both places with a plate and a small bowl, so that you and your companion can mix together oil, lemon juice, salt and pepper as the will takes you. Dip the raw vegetables into the dip, stir them around and eat.

Potato Pizza with Anchovies, Mascarpone and Rocket

Home-made pizzas are a real treat, and a cheap one too. They beat most takeaway pizzas hands down. This one is right up there at the top of the smart pizza list, with not a drop of tomato sauce in sight. Since the rest of the ingredients are incredibly cheap, you can afford to splash out on mascarpone, anchovies and fresh green rocket, which wilts a little in the heat of the pizza, giving a wonderful combination of peppery freshness and softened greens.

1 large potato (about 300 g/10 oz)
6 tinned anchovy fillets, cut in half lengthways
3 tablespoons mascarpone cheese
olive oil
85–100 g (3–3½ oz) rocket
salt and pepper

For the dough

400 g (14 oz) strong white bread flour
2 level teaspoons salt
1 sachet of easy-blend yeast
2 tablespoons olive oil

To make the dough, mix the flour, salt and yeast together in a bowl and make a well in the centre. Add the olive oil and enough water to mix to a soft, very slightly sticky dough – anything from 150–300 ml (¼–½ pint). Flour your hands and then gather your dough up into a ball. Knead vigorously on a lightly floured work surface for a good 8–10 minutes, until satin smooth and elastic (or use the dough hook of an electric mixer, at a low speed). Rinse the bowl out, then dry it and dust with flour. Place the dough in the bowl, turn to coat lightly in the flour, then cover with a damp cloth and leave in a warm place for about an hour or until it has doubled in size.

Peel the potato, then slice it paper thin either in a food processor or on a mandoline. This is the key to the pizza – if the potato is too thick it will not have time to cook through. Drop the potato slices into a bowl of cold water until needed.

Pre-heat the oven to 240°C/475°F/Gas Mark 9 or as high as it will go. Put 2 baking sheets in the oven to heat through. Return to the dough and punch it down. Gather up and knead again for a few minutes. Divide in half. Using your hands and/or a rolling pin, stretch the first ball of dough out to form a circle 25 cm (10 inches) across. When it is about right, use your fingers to push the dough to the edges, forming a thick rim. Lay the dough on a well-floured cold, flat baking sheet or even a sheet of strong cardboard, as long as it is amply floured. Arrange half the potato slices over the pizza, leaving the rim bare. Lay half the anchovies randomly on top, then dot half the mascarpone around, in teaspoonfuls. Season liberally, then drizzle a thin trickle of olive oil over the top. Repeat with the remaining dough and topping ingredients.

Open the oven and carefully shake and slide the pizzas on to the hot baking sheets inside. Bake for 10–15 minutes, until the edges are lightly tanned and the potatoes are beginning to brown. Take out of the oven and quickly divide the rocket between the pizzas, piling it casually over the surface. Drizzle over a last shot of olive oil, grind a little pepper over the top and then serve, with the rocket just beginning to soften here and there in the heat.

Lemon Mascarpone Ice-cream with Strawberry Coulis

This is inspired by a Venetian speciality called a *sgroppino*, which hovers half way between a pudding and a cocktail. A true *sgroppino* is a blend of lemon ice-cream, strawberry purée and the Venetian dry sparkling wine, prosecco, all whisked together to a marvellous slush. The prosecco, unfortunately, would have pushed the price of this menu way beyond the limit, but this lemon and mascarpone ice-cream is just superb with its own strawberry coulis merely spooned over the top.

45 g (1½ oz) caster sugar
finely grated zest and juice of 1 large lemon (about 60 ml (2 fl oz) juice)
250 g (9 oz) tub of mascarpone, less the 3 tablespoons needed for the pizzas (i.e. about 185 g/6½ oz) (see opposite)

For the coulis
150 g (5 oz) strawberries, hulled
10–20 g (⅓–⅔ oz) icing sugar
a dash of lemon juice

To make the ice-cream, put the sugar, half the lemon zest and 5 tablespoons of water into a pan. Stir over a moderate heat until the sugar has dissolved, then bring up to the boil and simmer for 2 minutes to make a syrup. Leave to cool.

Beat the lemon juice gradually into the mascarpone, adding the sugar syrup a little at a time until the mixture tastes just a touch on the sweet side (freezing always dulls the sweetness). Beat in the last of the lemon zest. If you have an ice-cream churn, freeze the mixture in that. If not, pour into a shallow container, cover and place in the freezer, turned to its lowest setting. When the sides have set (in my small freezer this takes around 1 hour), take the ice-cream out of the freezer, break up the frozen bits and push them towards the centre. Return to the freezer and repeat once more. Now leave the ice-cream until it is just about set solid but not yet rock hard. Either scrape it into a food processor and process to a smooth mush or tip it into a bowl and beat with all your might to break up large ice crystals. As soon as it is done, pour it back into the container and return it to the freezer. If you can be bothered, it is no bad thing to go through this last process one more time for an even smoother ice-cream, but you can get away without.

To make the strawberry coulis, process the strawberries with icing sugar to taste and the lemon juice. Cover and chill until needed. About half an hour before serving, transfer the ice-cream to the fridge to soften slightly.

To serve, divide the ice-cream between 2 beautiful stemmed glasses or sundae cups and then spoon over the strawberry coulis. Sheer, cooling, summertime bliss.

Following page (Clockwise from bottom left): Potato Pizza with Anchovies, Mascarpone and Rocket; Potato Pizza with Anchovies and Mascarpone (no rocket); Pinzimonio; Lemon Mascarpone Ice-cream with Strawberry Coulis

9

Fresh-as-a-daisy menu for four

Umbrian Panzanella

Raj Fishcakes with **Spring Onion** and **Coriander Mayonnaise**

Raspberry Sorbet with **Lace Biscuits**

I'm going to have to come clean. The only way that I could squeeze this meal out of a fiver was by including only half the cost of the lace biscuits. It's not an entirely unreasonable proposition, since the recipe makes at least 25 biscuits, and even though they are desperately moreish I felt that three per person was probably enough for one sitting. The big bonus is that you will have another dozen or so left over for tea.

I really didn't want to cut any corners, or pennies, from the other recipes, since I have a particular fondness for this menu. The food tastes wonderfully fresh and lively, although it incorporates stale bread, leftover cooked potatoes and possibly frozen fish. Thrifty, without a doubt, but all the better for that. And the bonus is that it comes with a real treat of a summery sorbet to finish the meal with great aplomb.

Umbrian Panzanella

The best-known version of the Italian salad panzanella is made with juicy, scarlet, high-summer tomatoes but several years ago, when I was working in Umbria, just below Tuscany, I came across this version without a tomato in sight but every bit as good. Both salads are made with stale bread, soaked to soften it, then stirred into the salad to give substance and flavour. Naturally, the bread needs to be of good quality (sliced white will not do), and the more flavour it has, the better. Last time I made it I used a stale loaf of shop-bought wholemeal, which worked very well. The idea is that the bread disintegrates into damp crumbs that spread evenly through the carrot and celery.

1 thick slice of stale bread (weighing about 60 g (2 oz) after the crusts have been removed)

2 celery stalks, finely diced

2 carrots, finely diced

½ fennel bulb, finely diced

½ red onion, finely diced

4 tablespoons olive oil

1 tablespoon red wine vinegar

6–8 basil leaves, roughly torn up

salt and pepper

Tear the bread up into pieces and place in a bowl. Sprinkle fairly generously with water and leave to soften for 5–10 minutes. Squeeze excess water out with your hands, mushing the bread up as you do so, then mix with all the remaining ingredients. Cover and leave at room temperature for an hour or so before serving. Stir well, then eat.

Raj Fishcakes

Usually fishcakes are made with something like salmon or smoked haddock, in other words a fish that has a moderately assertive and very appealing flavour. It's an excellent way of stretching a small amount of costly fish, or leftovers from a grander meal. Here, though, I'm starting off with a lesser fish. I used coley, which is not renowned for its fine flavour, and to make up for its lack of character I've given the fishcakes a good splash of Eastern spice. My panel of hungry testers, including one very fussy husband, gave the end result the thumbs up, clearing their plates enthusiastically. Any fresh, flaky white fish will do but don't be tempted into buying fish that is tired-looking, old and possibly a bit whiffy. That's a false economy. Far better, if that is all that is on offer, to turn to the freezer section and buy frozen fillets.

To make the fishcakes even nicer, though it will inevitably push you a few pence over the £5 limit, dip them into flour, then beaten egg and finally coat in fine breadcrumbs, before frying. Let the coating set in the fridge, then fry as normal for a crisp, crunchy coating.

300g (10 oz) coley, or whiting, ling, pout or any other cheap white fish fillets

1 small onion, finely chopped

3 tablespoons sunflower oil

1½ teaspoons ground cumin

1 teaspoon ground coriander

1 teaspoon mustard seeds

1 red chilli, deseeded and finely chopped

1 garlic clove, finely chopped

1 cm (½ inch) fresh root ginger, finely chopped

300g (10 oz) cooked potatoes, mashed

1 egg, beaten

salt and pepper

Steam, poach or microwave the fish until just cooked enough to flake. Flake the flesh, discarding the skin and any bones, and set aside. Fry the onion gently in 1 tablespoon of the oil until tender, without browning. Raise the heat and add the cumin, coriander and mustard seeds. Fry until the mustard seeds begin to pop and splutter. Now add the chilli, garlic and ginger and fry for another minute or so. Mix with the fish, mashed potatoes, salt, pepper and just enough beaten egg to bind.

Divide the mixture into 4 and shape into firm, round patties about 2.5cm (1 inch) thick. Chill for half an hour or more before cooking.

To cook, heat the remaining oil in a large frying pan over a moderate heat. Place the fishcakes in the pan and fry for about 4 minutes on each side, until browned. Serve with Spring Onion and Coriander Mayonnaise (see page 46).

Spring Onion and Coriander Mayonnaise

If you are lucky enough to live near an Asian or Cypriot grocery you can buy bunches of coriander for very little. A few tablespoons of chopped coriander, along with the mild onion flavour of spring onions, make a big difference to plain mayonnaise. Home-made mayo will taste best, but if you don't have the time or the inclination to whisk some up, turn to a jar of ready-made instead.

6 tablespoons mayonnaise (see page 28)
2 tablespoons chopped coriander
2 spring onions, thinly sliced

Mix all the ingredients together and serve.

Raspberry Sorbet

Summer is definitely the time of year to make sorbets. All those soft fruits are at their best and most prolific. Even if you can't make it to a pick-your-own farm, markets should be a good source of raspberries, strawberries and the like, especially at the end of the day when they are often sold off cheaply.

This raspberry sorbet is simplicity itself – just sieved raspberries, a little lemon juice and sugar syrup, all mixed up together. Once in the freezer, you have to pay it a little attention every now and then, but it's only a matter of a few minutes. The result pays handsomely for the small effort.

450 g (1 lb) raspberries
110 g (4 oz) sugar
150 ml (¼ pint) water
juice of ½ lemon

Push the raspberries through a sieve and set aside. Put the sugar and water into a pan and stir over a medium heat until the sugar has completely dissolved. Bring up to the boil and draw off the heat. Leave to cool.

Mix the sieved raspberries with the lemon juice and enough of the sugar syrup to sweeten to taste, bearing in mind that the cold of the freezer will dampen the sweetness to a small degree. If you have an ice-cream maker, churn the mixture in that. If not, pour it into a shallow container and place in the freezer, turned to its lowest setting. Leave until the sides have frozen solid but the centre is still runny – in my small freezer this takes about 1 hour. Take out of the freezer, break up the sides and push them into the middle. Return the sorbet to the fridge and leave until frozen solid but not yet rock hard. Scrape into a food processor and process to a slush. If you have no processor, then scrape the mixture into a bowl and beat hard and swiftly to a slush. The idea is to break down all the jagged ice crystals. Pour the slush back into the container and return to the freezer. If you have the patience, repeat this last step once more – not absolutely necessary but it does make for a smoother finish.

About half an hour before you want to eat the sorbet, transfer from the freezer to the fridge to allow it to soften.

Lace Biscuits

These are just the most terrific biscuits – crisp, sweet, buttery, lacy and elegant. Who would have thought that rolled oats could turn out quite so fancy? I make them frequently to go with puddings, or for presents, or just to nibble with coffee or at teatime. These quantities make loads of biscuits, at least 25 if not more, so store the ones you're not going to eat at the first sitting in an airtight container to keep their crunch.

110 g (4 oz) rolled oats
1 tablespoon plain flour, sifted
225 g (8 oz) caster sugar
¼ teaspoon salt
110 g (4 oz) butter
1 large egg, lightly beaten
¼ teaspoon vanilla essence

Pre-heat the oven to 170°C/325°F/Gas Mark 3.
Line several baking sheets with non-stick baking
parchment.

Mix the oats, flour, sugar and salt together. Melt the
butter and pour it over the dry ingredients while it is
still hot. Stir until evenly mixed. Make a well in the
centre and add the egg and vanilla essence. Mix
thoroughly. Drop teaspoons of the mixture on to the
baking sheets, leaving a good 5 cm (2 inch) gap
between each dollop. Bake for 10–12 minutes, until
golden brown. Leave to cool on the baking sheets
for a few minutes, then transfer to wire racks to cool
completely.

10

Saving the *Sunshine*

Plum and **Walnut**
Jam

Tomato and **Runner**
Bean Relish

Giardiniera

Right through the summer, gluts of fruit and
vegetables bring prices down very low, especially in
markets. In fact, if you have friends with vegetable
gardens or allotments they'll probably be delighted
to pass some of their surplus on to you for free
if you'll do the picking, or a spot of weeding.
Of course, if you grow your own, you will already
know how seemingly endless the crop from just a
few plants can be. There are only so many runner
beans a family can eat in a matter of weeks. All that
fecund excess makes this the very best time of
year to brew up home-made preserves. Not only
will they be cheaper than all but the lowliest of
shop-made jams and chutneys, they will also taste
infinitely better. Here are three of my favourites to
get you going, each one costing far less than a
fiver to make.

Plum and Walnut Jam

My mother used to make plum and walnut jam and to this day I think it is one of the great combinations. It's a late-summer preserve, to be made as the season is drawing to a close and trees are laden with fat, purple Victorias and other types of luscious plums. Later on, look out in the hedgerows for smaller, sour damsons – too astringent to eat raw but marvellous in crumbles and pies and, of course, made into jam.

Make sure you use fruit that is either a little underripe or just ripe but still firm. Discard bruised, softened bits as these will shorten the shelf-life of the jam something rotten. You can cook the plums whole, removing the stones with a slotted spoon as they rise to the surface, but I prefer to halve and stone them before adding them to the pan, especially when they come from our trees, or a neighbour's garden. All too often they house tiny worms, and though these would do no one any harm after being boiled into jam, I nonetheless prefer to cut them out of the plums before cooking!

Makes about 2.75 kg (6 lb)

2 kg (4½ lb) plums (or 1.6 kg (3½ lb) damsons)
600 ml (1 pint) water
2 kg (4½ lb) granulated sugar
15 g (½ oz) butter
250 g (9 oz) walnut pieces

Halve the plums and discard the stones and any damaged or wormy bits. Put the prepared plums into a preserving pan or a large, heavy saucepan. Add the water and bring up to the boil. Reduce the heat and simmer very gently for about half an hour, until the plums are very soft and the level has gone down by about one third.

Meanwhile, warm the sugar through in a low oven or a warm airing cupboard. Once the plums are cooked, tip in the sugar and stir until completely dissolved, without letting the mixture boil. When the sugar has dissolved, stir in the butter, then bring back to the boil. Boil hard for about 10–15 minutes, until setting point is reached (see page 124). Draw the pan off the heat and skim off any scum from the surface of the jam. Stir in the walnuts and ladle into hot sterilized jars (see page 124). Cover the surface with waxed discs, then seal, label and leave to cool. Store in a cool, dark, dry cupboard.

Tomato and Runner Bean Relish

Last summer it seemed as if runner beans were out to get me. Everywhere I went I stumbled across mountains of them for sale – in shops, markets and on tables set up by the roadside. Whenever I visited friends with vegetable patches they offered me a bag of runner beans to take home, but then that was just what we were doing when we had visitors. I have to admit that runner beans are not my all-time top vegetable, especially when they are spectacularly large and tough, but now and again I do appreciate their distinctive, squeaky-firm texture. It seems even better, however, when transformed into a relish like this one, spiced with cumin, sweetened with raisins and given extra crunch with sunflower seeds.

Like most chutneys and cooked relishes, this one improves with age. When first made it tastes rather vinegary and crude, but give it a fortnight in the jar and it will have mellowed quite remarkably. Time smoothes out the rough edges. It goes very well with cheese or cold meats, and is just dandy with burgers or barbecued sausages.

Makes about 2.75 kg (6 lb)

900 g (2 lb) runner beans, topped and tailed
1.5 kg (3 lb) tomatoes, skinned and roughly chopped
2 large onions, chopped
350 ml (12 fl oz) red wine vinegar or cider vinegar
175 g (6 oz) raisins or sultanas
85 g (3 oz) sunflower seeds
340 g (12 oz) granulated sugar
½ tablespoon allspice berries (pimento), coarsely crushed
1 teaspoon ground ginger
1 tablespoon cumin seeds
6 cloves
15 g (½ oz) black mustard seeds

Pull any strings away from the sides of the runner beans. Cut them in half lengthways, then slice across the strips to make small dice. Put into a preserving pan or a large, heavy saucepan with the tomatoes, onion and 3 tablespoons of the vinegar. Cook gently for about 10 minutes, stirring frequently. Now add the remaining vinegar and all the rest of the ingredients. Bring up to the boil, then simmer gently for 40–50 minutes, until very thick. Ladle into hot, sterilized jars (see page 124), seal with non-corrosive lids and then label. Store for at least 2 weeks in a cool, dark, dry cupboard before eating.

Giardiniera

This is an Italian mixed vegetable preserve and the exact mix is really up to you. It all depends on what you can lay your hands on, and what you fancy. A generous assortment of colours, flavours and textures will give you the best of all worlds, so use my suggestions as a rough guide, and try your hand at it. The vegetables are cooked first in a mildly vinegary bath to soften and sharpen them up, then submerged in oil to preserve and enrich them.

Makes enough for a 1 litre (1¾ pint) preserving jar

2 onions, peeled and quartered
225 g (8 oz) carrots, cut into batons about 1 cm (½ inch) thick and 5 cm (2 inches) long
225 g (8 oz) cauliflower florets, broken into pieces no more than 2.5 cm (1 inch) across
225 g (8 oz) runner beans, thinly sliced, or green beans, halved
1 red and 1 green pepper, cut into strips 1 cm (½ inch) wide and 5 cm (2 inches) long
600 ml (1 pint) white wine vinegar
900 ml (1½ pints) water
1 tablespoon sugar
1 bay leaf
½ tablespoon peppercorns
½ tablespoon coriander seeds
2 sprigs of thyme
about 300 ml (½ pint) each extra virgin olive oil and sunflower or corn oil

Keep all the vegetables in separate heaps. Put the vinegar into a preserving pan or a large, heavy non-reactive saucepan with the water, sugar, bay leaf, peppercorns, coriander seeds and thyme and bring up to the boil. Add the onions, carrots and cauliflower, bring back to the boil, and simmer for 5 minutes. Add the runner beans or green beans and the peppers and simmer for 4–5 minutes or until all the vegetables are just about tender. Drain them thoroughly and dry on kitchen paper or in a clean tea towel. Leave to cool.

Pack the vegetables into a large sterilized preserving jar (see page 124). Mix the two oils and pour over enough to cover the vegetables completely. You may find you need a little less or a little more than the full amount. Tap the jar gently on the work surface to expel any trapped air bubbles, then if necessary top up the oil level so that the vegetables are completely covered. Seal tightly and leave in a cool, dark place for at least 2 weeks, preferably a month, before dipping in.

AUTUMN

Harvest *Supper* in Brixton

'We plough the fields and scatter
The good seed on the land,
But it is fed and watered,
By God's almighty hand.'

When it comes to celebrating the safe gathering in of the harvest at the end of September, most of us think of the countryside: the golden fields of wheat now cut down to scratchy stubble, orchards full of plums and apples and pears, rows of marrows, leeks and cabbages, and the very last vestiges of the summer's delirious crop.

The harvest festival may conjure up rural idylls but it is honoured throughout cities and towns with just as much fervour as in the country. After all, we have much to be thankful for, whether it be the provisions at the local greengrocer's or supermarket, or freshly picked greenery from the allotment or market garden.

So it was with great anticipation that I left my little patch of rural idyll towards the end of September and headed off to South London to join in the preparations for a fantastic harvest supper, Brixton style. By the time I arrived at the Kenyon Baptist Church, work was in full and noisy progress. Behind the church, in the kitchens of the church hall, I found Helena, Brenda and Walter, amongst others, beavering away merrily on their own particular contribution to the supper. They had sold more than 100 tickets to members of the congregation at the princely sum of £5 per head, so it was all hands to the deck. The food they prepare is thoroughly, vigorously Caribbean in style, full of electric flavours and solid reassuring comfort.

In exchange for a few lessons in Caribbean cooking, I volunteered to create a vegetarian main course and a sumptuous pudding that wouldn't break the bank. The deal was on, and I rushed out to the babbling, thronged, bustling streets around Electric Avenue, home of Brixton's renowned market. Inspiration lay in wait for me by the sackful. Glorious pumpkins and squashes, sweet potatoes and yams, limes and lemons, hot, hot, hot chillies, bunches of wiry, fragrant thyme, piles of spring onions – or scallions as they are labelled here – sweetcorn, and new season's apples. The fish stalls are a riot of colour with great heaps of exotic fish curling alongside the more familiar specimens like cod and conger. I laid in my provisions and splashed out on stunning rainbow-coloured hairpieces to take home to my four-year-old daughter for her dressing-up box. What a fabulous haul.

Saturday night came all too quickly, and amidst the laying of tables and the decorating of the hall the activity in the kitchens rose to fever pitch. By some small miracle (or was it just unperceived Immaculate organization ...) the preparations drew to a close as the tables filled. A few hymns and the address by the Pastor heralded the meal itself – a triumph on all counts, and stunningly good value by anyone's standards. With stomachs finally filled to each and everyone's satisfaction, more rousing singing broke out and, all too soon, the evening drew to a close. What better way than this marvellous feast to remember and give thanks for the food we take for granted throughout so much of the year?

Though I've cut down on quantities in the recipes that follow, the value remains true to form. Celebrate your own harvest supper at home with the spices and vivid flavours that conjure up the warmth of the Caribbean.

1

A light *lunch* for the workers (for four)

Escoveitched Red Snapper, Bread

Brown Sugar Lemonade

It's all too easy when you are working hard to forget to eat – even when you are preparing a meal for 100 and more. One of the small contributions I could make to the harvest supper was to keep the band of workers fed and watered. The red snapper in the market proved incredibly good value, so I bore them off to my borrowed kitchen to make a classic Jamaican dish, escoveitched fish – in other words, marinated fried fish. With thick slices of good bread, and chilled lemonade to wash it all down, it hit the spot instantly, reviving flagging spirits and eliciting, I was relieved to hear, considerable approval.

Even if you are not engrossed in some huge task, this makes an excellent light lunch, especially on a warm day. The marinated fish will keep in the fridge for three or four days, as will the lemonade, so it can be prepared well in advance. You might want to add a simple green salad, or even a tomato salad when British tomatoes are at their cheapest from August through to the end of September.

Escoveitched Red Snapper

The word 'escoveitched' comes from the same roots as escabeche in Spain and Latin America, scapece in Italy and caveach in the UK. Each of these countries and regions has its own particular version, but what it boils down to is a dish of fried fish (or, in some instances, meat or vegetables) that is then soused in a piquant marinade and served cold. There's even a Japanese version, borrowed from the Portuguese. In the pre-refrigeration past, this method was an excellent way of extending the shelf-life of a highly perishable commodity but now, when fridges are commonplace, fish is escoveitched mainly because it tastes so good. The marinade is what bears the signature of the country, and in Jamaica it includes, of course, a red-hot Scotch bonnet chilli – although to be fair the finished dish is not too fiery – and that characteristic spice, allspice or pimento berries.

continued on page 56

Following page
(From left to right):
Escoveitched Red
Snapper, Bread;
Brown Sugar Lemonade

continued from page 53

When you see good-quality fresh fish on special offer it's worth buying enough to cook that day for lunch or supper, and then more to 'escoveitch' for a day or two or even three later. Red snapper is the fish that's preferred in Jamaica – and in Brixton, where it can be bought at a good price in Electric Avenue market – but any other relatively small fish can be used instead. I've tried it with trout, mackerel and plenty of others besides.

juice of 2 limes
4 red snappers, filleted
sunflower or vegetable oil for frying
salt and pepper

For the marinade

300 ml (½ pint) cane vinegar or white wine vinegar
150 ml (¼ pint) water
1 Scotch bonnet chilli, deseeded and cut into rings
1 chayote, or cucumber, peeled and cut into long strips
1 red pepper, deseeded and cut into long strips (optional)
2 onions, sliced
2 bay leaves
1 cm (½ inch) fresh root ginger, sliced
1 garlic clove, sliced
12 allspice (pimento) berries

Begin by rubbing the lime juice into the fish fillets, then season with salt and pepper. Set aside for 30 minutes. Meanwhile, put all the ingredients for the marinade in a saucepan and bring up to the boil, then reduce the heat and simmer until the onions are tender (about 15 minutes). Reheat if necessary, when you are ready to use it.

Fill a wide frying pan with oil to a depth of 1 cm (½ inch) and heat until very hot. Dry the snapper on kitchen paper or a clean tea towel. Fry in hot, hot oil, allowing about 1–2 minutes on each side, until patched with brown. Don't overcrowd the pan or you'll reduce the temperature too much and the fish will stick mercilessly. Lift out carefully and arrange in a shallow dish. Pour the hot marinade over the fish and leave to marinate for at least 2 hours before serving, with thick slices of bread.

Brown Sugar Lemonade

I've always made my lemonade with white sugar but the ladies of Kenyon Baptist Church shake their heads at this notion. 'I always use demerara,' says Helena firmly. So, demerara it is, but done my way, in the food processor.

4 lemons
2 limes
about 200 g (7 oz) demerara sugar
ice cubes
a few sprigs of mint

Slice the ends off the lemons and limes and discard. Cut the citrus fruit up roughly and put into a food processor with any juice that has squeezed out under the knife blade. Add about 110 g (4 oz) of the demerara sugar and 300 ml (½ pint) water. Process to a mush, then tip out into a sieve set over a bowl. Press down (but don't try to rub the lemon mush through or it will taste horribly bitter) to extract the last few drops of liquid, then return the contents of the sieve to the processor with 60 g (2 oz) sugar and another 300 ml (½ pint) water and repeat the whole process. Pop the debris back into the processor, add 150 ml (¼ pint) water and about 30 g (1 oz) demerara sugar and process one last time. Strain again, pressing down to extract the last few drops of fragrant juice, then discard all the debris in the sieve. Taste the lemonade and, if it is still too sharp, add more water and stir in a little more sugar. Serve chilled, with clinking ice cubes and sprigs of mint.

A taste of the *Caribbean* for four

Potato and **Marrow Soup**

Walter's Jerk Pork

Fricassée Chicken

Rice and **Peas**

This is a selection of dishes from the Kenyon Baptist Church's harvest supper. The first course was straightforward – just small bowls of steaming-hot vegetable soup. This was followed by an almost impossible multiple choice of main courses. Luckily every choice was a good one, and the two I've included here are particularly appealing. Both need the soothing nature of that famous Jamaican accompaniment, rice and peas, to tame their spicy hearts. On the tables were simple salads of sliced cucumber, tomato, lettuce and spring onion to bring the temperature down even more. With such big numbers to cater for (they cook for at least 100 hungry guests), they can buy the meat from wholesalers for a very low price, which means they can afford to round off the meal with fruit flans as well. When you cut the guest list down to a mere four the price is relatively high, which means pudding is out of the question unless you are prepared to break the budget. If you do fancy a touch of sweetness after the meal, flick through this book to find plenty of puddings that won't take the bill too far over a fiver.

And another home note – choose one or other of the main courses, not both. You can't expect miracles, even at this time of year.

Potato and Marrow Soup

This is a soothing, gentle soup made with ingredients that should cost you next to nothing. Thyme, used plentifully to scent the soup, provides the echo of West Indian cooking.

30 g (1 oz) butter
1 small onion, chopped
1 large carrot, chopped
450 g (1 lb) peeled deseeded marrow, diced
340 g (12 oz) peeled potato, diced
1 garlic clove, chopped
a small bunch of thyme, tied together with string
1 litre (1¾ pints) vegetable or chicken stock
salt and pepper
chopped chives or parsley, to serve

Melt the butter in a fairly large saucepan. Add all the vegetables, as well as the garlic and thyme. Stir, then cover and leave to sweat over a low heat for 10 minutes, stirring once or twice. Pour in the stock and bring up to the boil. Season with salt and pepper, then simmer for about 20 minutes, until all the vegetables are very tender. Remove the bunch of thyme. Liquidize the soup in several batches, then return it to the pan, adding extra stock if required to thin it down. Taste and adjust the seasoning.

Bring back to the boil and then serve, sprinkled with chives or parsley.

Walter's Jerk Pork

Walter is rising 70 and the life and soul of the party. Always joking and teasing gently, he is renowned throughout the community for his special jerk pork. He makes it for all the big occasions and this one was no exception. Walter's jerk pork just had to be on the menu. I can't say that this is exactly his recipe, since I replaced some of the particular blends of Caribbean seasoning spices he buys with more widely available choices, but it is based very closely on Walter's special. Walter used a Caribbean seasoning salt but the nearest I could find in supermarkets near me was an American seasoning salt bearing the name of the Louisiana chef, Paul Prudhomme. If you can find a jar of jerk seasoning paste, add a couple of teaspoonfuls of that to the mixture as well.

The final dish of pork has a strong, deep, hot flavour, and the meat is meltingly tender. Serve it with rice and peas.

Serves 4–6

2 tablespoons sunflower oil or other bland oil	
1 kg (2¼ lb) belly pork	

To season the pork

1 teaspoon salt	
3 garlic cloves, crushed	
1 teaspoon seasoning salt	
1 tablespoon whole allspice (pimento berries), roughly crushed	
1 tablespoon freshly ground black pepper	
3 dried bay leaves, roughly crumbled	
1 tablespoon soy sauce	
1 tablespoon very hot chilli sauce	

Mix all the dry seasoning ingredients together and rub well into the pork. Shake over the soy sauce and chilli sauce, then leave for an hour or more.

Pre-heat the oven to 200°C/400°F/Gas Mark 6.

Pour the oil into a roasting tin just large enough to take the pork. Heat through in the oven for 5–10 minutes. Take out and immediately put the pork into the hot oil. Turn with a fork or tongs so that both sides are coated in oil, then cover with foil. Return to the oven and leave to sweat and sizzle for 1 hour, until the pork is so tender that a fork slides through it like softened butter. Uncover and raise the heat to its highest level. Bake for another 10–15 minutes, until nicely coloured. Serve hot, warm or cold.

Fricassée Chicken

Fricassée chicken, a spicy dark stew, is one of the characteristic dishes of the Caribbean, and also just happens to be Helena's speciality. Of course, the method varies not only from island to island but also from cook to cook. This is her tried-and-tested method.

The sliced Scotch bonnet chilli will release heat into the fricassée, so how much you use depends on how hot you like your chicken. The whole Scotch bonnet is more to do with flavour than searing heat, but it does provide a modicum of chilli fire even though the skin is never broken (be careful when stirring ...).

juice of 1 lemon

a 1–1.5 kg (2¼ lb–3 lb) chicken, cut into 8 pieces

1 tablespoon sunflower or vegetable oil

2 onions, finely chopped

2 spring onions, chopped

3 tomatoes, skinned, deseeded and chopped

450 ml (¾ pint) chicken stock

1 whole Scotch bonnet chilli

1 bay leaf

salt and pepper

chopped parsley, to garnish (optional)

For the marinade

3 garlic cloves, crushed

1 tablespoon white wine vinegar

1 tablespoon Worcestershire sauce

1 teaspoon salt

1 teaspoon dried thyme

2 teaspoons freshly ground black pepper

¼ teaspoon ground allspice (pimento)

3–4 slices of Scotch bonnet chilli, deseeded

Rub the lemon juice all over the chicken pieces. Mix all the marinade ingredients together. Place the chicken in a large mixing bowl and spoon the marinade over it. Turn the chicken to make sure that it is thoroughly coated, then cover and leave to marinate in the fridge for at least 2 hours and up to 24 hours, turning the pieces occasionally.

Remove the chicken from the marinade and dry with kitchen paper. Reserve the marinade.

In a large saucepan or, better still, a wok, which is what Helena uses, heat the oil until very hot. Add the chicken, 4 pieces at a time, and brown thoroughly on both sides. Remove the chicken from the pan and drain off the oil. Return the pan to the heat and, using 1 tablespoon of the oil, fry the chopped onions and spring onions until tender. Now add the tomatoes and cook down to a thick, dark mush. Return the chicken to the pan and add the stock and the reserved marinade (with or without the slices of chilli, depending on the degree of fire you desire), the whole Scotch bonnet and the bay leaf. Bring to the boil and simmer for about 40 minutes, until the chicken is cooked through.

Adjust the seasoning to taste. Discard the whole Scotch bonnet and sprinkle with parsley, if you wish. Serve the fricassée with Rice and Peas (see below), or plain boiled rice.

Rice and Peas

110 g (4 oz) dried pigeon peas, or black-eyed beans or red kidney beans

300 g (10 oz) long grain rice

3 spring onions, chopped

60 g (2 oz) creamed coconut, grated or chopped

15 g (½ oz) butter

salt

Pigeon peas and black-eyed beans need no soaking. Kidney beans will need to be soaked overnight. Put the beans, drained if they have been soaked, into a large pan with plenty of water (and no salt at this stage), then bring up to the boil. Boil hard for 15 minutes, then reduce the heat and simmer until the beans are tender. Drain and set them aside.

Cook the rice in salted water until almost tender but still slightly chalky in the centre, then drain. Mix the rice with the beans, spring onions and creamed coconut. Now rinse the pan out and pour in enough water just to cover the base and no more. Tip the rice mixture in and dot with the butter. Lay a clean tea towel over the top, then cover with the lid, so that you have a very snug fit, lifting the trailing ends of cloth up over the lid so that they don't go up in flames. Cook over a low heat for 5 minutes or so, to steam the rice until perfectly tender. Fluff the rice up with a fork, then taste and adjust the seasoning.

A harvest *feast* for eight to ten

Pumpkin, Sweetcorn and **Sweet Potato Stew**

Angel Food Cake and **Custard**

Blackberry and **Apple Compote** with **Star Anise**

The dishes that make up this menu are the ones that I contributed to the Brixton harvest supper. They make the most of all the marvellous produce that is around at this special time of year, when summer is receding and the leaves are turning golden to welcome in the autumn. I'll admit to a slight cheat here – even if you do lay your hands on a free marrow, which shouldn't be too difficult, and pick your own blackberries from the brambles, the cost still hovers nearer to a tenner than a fiver, though there is enough to satisfy 8–10 people in all. I'm justifying its inclusion on the basis that it costs less than £5 to feed four people royally this way – it's just that it's almost impossible to cook these dishes in small quantity. Well, that's my story and I'm sticking to it.

Pumpkin, Sweetcorn and Sweet Potato Stew

This is a big stew, full of the orange and yellow hues of autumn, rich with coconut milk and toasted spices. Served in the pumpkin shell, it looks tremendous and feeds a crowd. It happens to be meat-free, so should your crowd include vegetarians it is just the ticket.

If you can buy the vegetables in the market, rather than at a more expensive supermarket, you can land yourself with a real bargain. Serve the stew with rice (though I usually prefer white, this is one instance where the nutty flavour of brown rice would work particularly well) and it makes a substantial main course. The stew can be made in advance and reheated when needed.

1 medium-large pumpkin

45 g (1½ oz) butter

45 g (1½ oz) light muscovado sugar

1½ teaspoons cinnamon

1 tablespoon coriander seeds

1½ tablespoons cumin seeds

1 dried red chilli, snapped into 2 or 3 pieces

1 tablespoon dried oregano

2 large onions, chopped

5 garlic cloves, chopped

3 tablespoons sunflower oil

400 g (14 oz) tin of tomatoes, roughly chopped,
with their juice

1 tablespoon tomato purée

1 tablespoon Worcestershire sauce

Tabasco to taste

300 ml (½ pint) apple juice

600 ml (1 pint) water

650 g (1½ lb) sweet potatoes, peeled and cut into
2.5 cm (1 inch) cubes

650 g (1½ lb) potatoes, peeled and cut into
2.5 cm (1 inch) cubes

1 small marrow, peeled, deseeded and cut into
2.5 cm (1 inch) cubes

30 prunes (preferably with stones in)

340 g (12 oz) frozen sweetcorn kernels, thawed

425 ml (14 fl oz) coconut milk (see page 18)

4 tablespoons chopped coriander

salt and pepper

Pre-heat the oven to 180°C/350°F/Gas Mark 4.

To prepare the pumpkin, cut a lid off the top and scoop out the seeds with your hands, a spoon or whatever seems to work best for you. Now, using a sharp knife or a sturdy metal spoon, excavate the flesh, leaving a good solid wall of pumpkin. Try to extract at least 450–650 g (1–1½ lb), then chop roughly and reserve. Smear the butter all over the interior of the pumpkin. Mix the brown sugar and cinnamon and sprinkle and spread it around the interior. Sit the pumpkin in a buttered baking tray and bake for about 20 minutes, until slightly softened but still sturdy. Reheat when needed.

Now for the stew itself. First toast the spices, by dry-frying the coriander and cumin seeds in a heavy frying pan over a moderate heat for a couple of minutes. When they are beginning to scent the room, add the chilli and oregano and dry-fry for a further 30 seconds or so, shaking the pan constantly. Tip into a cold bowl and allow to cool for a few minutes before grinding to a fine powder. Reserve.

Fry the onions and garlic in the oil in a great big casserole or saucepan (I use my preserving pan), without letting them brown. When they are tender, add the spices and stir about for a minute. Now add the tinned tomatoes, tomato purée, Worcestershire sauce, a small shake of Tabasco, the apple juice and the water. Bring up to the boil and simmer for 10 minutes. Next add both kinds of potato and the pumpkin flesh. Simmer for another 20–30 minutes or so, until the pumpkin has dissolved to thicken the juices and the potatoes are almost tender. Now add the marrow, prunes, sweetcorn and coconut milk. Stir in well, then leave for a final 15 minutes' simmering. Taste and adjust the seasoning, adding more Tabasco if you fancy a more striking blast of heat.

Shortly before serving, reheat the pumpkin in the oven, at the same temperature as before, for about 15 minutes. Reheat the stew, too. Nestle the pumpkin in a large bowl that will give it a bit of additional support and then fill with the stew (it probably won't all fit in, so keep the rest warm and refill the pumpkin when needed. Scatter over a little fresh coriander, and then scatter a little more on each bowl as you serve.

Following page
(Clockwise from front):
Pumpkin, Sweetcorn and
Sweet Potato Stew; Angel
Food Cake and Custard;
Blackberry and Apple
Compote with Star Anise

Angel Food Cake

A cake that is pure, white and light enough for angels. This is a wonderful American creation and, incidentally, a brilliant cake for anyone who is on a low-fat diet, since it contains absolutely no fat whatsoever. In texture it is quite unlike an ordinary cake, sort of bouncier and stickier, but not moist exactly. Anyway, I love it on its own, with a cup of tea or coffee, or better still as a pudding, served with a compote of seasonal fruit and a slick of primrose-yellow custard (which instantly destroys any pretence at low-fat saintliness ...).

If you don't want to make a vat of custard to go with it, you can either freeze egg whites one by one and wait until you have enough to make this cake, or you can make it anyway and freeze the egg yolks until you have need of them.

Any left-over cake is delicious toasted for breakfast or tea, or as a light replacement for all those fancy puddings that employ a slice of toasted brioche as a base for fruit compotes, or butter-fried soft fruit and a dastardly indulgent wallop of mascarpone.

150 g (5 oz) plain flour
350 ml (12 fl oz) egg whites (around 10–12 large ones), with not a speck of yolk in them
¼ teaspoon salt
1 level teaspoon cream of tartar
1 tablespoon lemon juice
300 g (10 oz) caster sugar
1½ teaspoons vanilla essence

Pre-heat the oven to 180°C/350°F/Gas Mark 4.

Sift the flour 6 times, holding the sieve up high over the bowl, to make it as light and airy as possible. Whisk the egg whites in a very large bowl until they are foamy. Sprinkle over the salt, cream of tartar and lemon juice. Continue whisking until the mixture forms soft peaks. Now start adding the sugar gradually, along with the vanilla, whisking it in well every time until the whites form stiff peaks. Sift the flour over the mixture and fold in lightly. Pour into an ungreased 25 cm (10 inch) ring mould, smooth down lightly and bake for 50–55 minutes, until the cake springs back when gently pressed.

Now for the quaint part. The cake needs to cool upside down, with air circulating freely all around. Assuming you don't have a special angel food cake mould complete with legs, it can be balanced either on the edges of three tumblers or tins, or hanging over the neck of a bottle. When it is completely cool, carefully tease the sides of the cake away from the tin with a fork, loosening it gently until it comes out neatly.

When serving the cake, turn to forks again. Use 2 at a time to gently pull the cake apart. If you use a knife it gums up the edges and squishes them together in an ungainly and unappealing fashion.

Custard

When I make custard in small quantity I use nothing but egg yolks to thicken it, but for a big vat of custard to feed a crowd I prefer not to take any chances. By combining yolks and flour, you eliminate any risk of curdling the custard. In fact, it needs to be boiled (the one thing you absolutely can't do to a classic custard) to cook out the taste of raw flour.

Vanilla is the most common flavouring for custard but by no means the only one. Bay leaves give an unusual almondy flavour, while sweet cicely imparts a mildly aniseed taste.

10–12 egg yolks
110 g (4 oz) caster sugar
150 g (5 oz) plain flour
900 ml (1½ pints) milk
600 ml (1 pint) single cream (or milk, or milk mixed with cream, according to the budget)
5 bay leaves, a small bunch of sweet cicely, or 1½ teaspoons vanilla essence

Beat the egg yolks with the sugar. Add the flour and beat in smoothly. Put the milk, cream and flavouring in a pan and bring up to the boil slowly. Pour on to the egg yolk mixture, whisking constantly, then pour the mixture back into the pan. Bring up to the boil, stirring continuously. Simmer until slightly thickened, then strain into a cool bowl. Serve hot, warm or cold.

Blackberry and Apple Compote with Star Anise

Gather blackberries while the going is good in late summer and early autumn before the frosts perish them. To stretch them out a little, partner with new season's apples (eaters, not cookers, please) to make a wonderful old-fashioned blackberry and apple compote. I love the hint of aniseed imparted by the star anise, but they are entirely optional. Any left-over compote is lovely for breakfast, eaten with large dollops of Greek yoghurt.

900 g (2 lb) blackberries
10 good eating apples, peeled, cored and sliced
500 g (1 lb 2 oz) caster sugar
2 cinnamon sticks
2 star anise (or 4 cloves)

Put all the ingredients in a non-reactive saucepan and add about 60 ml (2 fl oz) water. Cover and cook over a low heat for 5 minutes, until the dark blackberry juice begins to ooze out, stirring once or twice to dissolve the sugar. Simmer until the slices of apple are very tender. Serve hot, warm or cold.

A Cold and Damp Weekend in *Northern Ireland*

Well, Ireland does have a reputation for rain and this weekend was no exception. The grey clouds rolled in as we landed in Belfast and stayed put until the moment we left again – and probably long after. Not that we minded too much, for we were on our way to one of the finest guesthouses in the whole of the island, north or south. Grange Lodge is almost as famous as Ireland's rain, and its proprietress, Norah Brown, is renowned throughout the North as an ambassador for the fine food that comes from the Emerald Isle.

A warm welcome and the scent of new-baked bread greeted us as we arrived. Norah, it turns out, is a consummate, masterly baker and, as anyone who lives in or has been to Ireland will tell you, the marvellous bread is one of the highlights of any meal taken there. Forget potatoes (not entirely, of course, for they too are very good here), it's the bread that I look forward to every time I visit. Norah's bread is especially good, and especially moreish. In fact, I'd probably have been quite happy with nothing else but bread and golden salty butter on the table all weekend long, but it was not to be. Late autumn, when the wind is turning bitter and the rains pelt down with the chill of impending winter, is the time when the last and perhaps the best of the autumn's harvest rolls in.

From the vegetable garden, Norah and I gathered in cannonball beetroot, not as elegantly flavoured as small spring and summer ones but not to be despised either. The first frosts had given the parsnips a superb sweetness, so we hauled in a few of those too, along with fat leeks, hefty carrots, flat-leaved parsley, onions and garlic.

In late autumn the last of the apples and pears are on sale – again often at knockdown prices in markets or straight from growers – and chestnuts are coming in to soften the edges of the chill. There's nothing nicer on a miserable dark evening than roasting sweet, mealy chestnuts over an open fire. Pumpkins and squashes, too, are big and sturdy, often sold off quickly once Bonfire Night is over.

Taking a fine brace of pheasant and the trugs of vegetables and fruit as our inspiration, we cooked up a storm in Norah's snug kitchen. Thirty-six hours and three meals later, I hung up the oven gloves and regretfully took my leave, armed with a sheaf of recipes from Norah and filled to the brim not just with food, but also with the cheerful, warm bonhomie that the Browns spread wherever they go.

How to skin a pheasant

The costing of the two menus that follow depends entirely on buying a brace of pheasant in feather and dealing with the business of removing those feathers yourself. Norah doesn't pluck, however. Oh no, far too messy and time-consuming. Skinning is Norah's way of short-circuiting the lengthy business of plucking a pheasant.
Be warned, however, that if you are squeamish it would probably be wise either to rope in a friend to do the dastardly deed or to give in, go for broke and stump up the extra cash for a brace of fully prepared birds. Having said that, I'd like to suggest that the rest of you give it a whirl, even if you are a touch hesitant. It's not difficult to do, it's not even that messy (and certainly not half as messy and time-consuming as plucking the birds), and it's mighty satisfying when the deed is done.

Norah tells me that when she's on her own she can skin a bird in four minutes flat ... but then she's been practising since she was a child. To be on the safe side, allow half an hour or so for the brace if you are a novice.

1 Open an old newspaper out flat on the table, and arm yourself with a sharp, short-bladed knife and a pair of poultry shears if you have them, though they are not essential. Take the first bird and cut off its feet at the 'knee' joints.

2 Open up each wing in turn and cut off the main wing, by slashing first through the skin into the inner joint to loosen it, then bending the wing back to crack open the joint, making it easy to slice through.

3 Turn the pheasant back up, breast down and stretch out the neck. Pull off a few handfuls of the feathers at the base of the neck, running from between the upper part of the wings and working about 5–7.5 cm (2–3 inches) up towards the head.

4 Using the tip of the knife, slit open the skin that has been exposed. With your fingers, pull it back and work your way round the neck, pulling it free from the skin. Use the poultry shears or the knife to cut the neck partly away from the body, and pull it to one side.

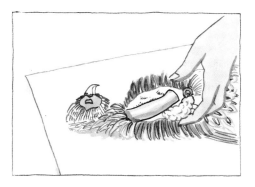

5 Underneath, nestled right into the base of the neck, you should be able to see, or at least feel the crop, which is where the bird stores its last feed of oats and other pheasanty treats. Tease it loose with your fingers and pull it away from the body, then cut through the last of the neck skin to remove the head and crop entirely from the body. Discard them.

6 Turn the pheasant over and pull a few more feathers away from the breastbone of the bird at the neck end, to expose bare skin.

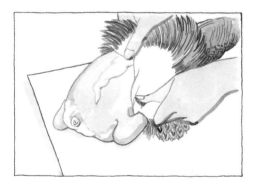

7 With the tip of the knife, make a small slit in the skin. Grasp the skin on both sides of the slit firmly in each hand and tug it away from the body to begin to loosen it. Turn the bird on one side and work the skin away from the body down over one of the wing stumps, as if undressing a tightly clad doll. Pull it right off to leave the wing clean. Turn the bird over to the other side and repeat.

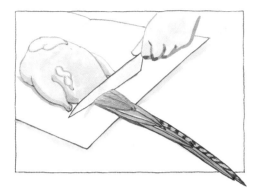

8 Now it's downhill all the way. Grasp the jacket of feathers and skin, pull it right down the rest of the body and slip it off, leaving just the tail feathers. Slice them off at the base and, hey presto, the bird is skinned. Repeat the task with the second pheasant.

For the following recipes, you must cut off both legs and breasts. To remove the legs, just bend them back one at a time, away from the body until the joint cracks open, then slice through. To cut off the breasts, slide a sharp knife down along the backbone on one side and work down, keeping the blade close to the bone, until you have completely released the plump lobe of breast meat, then do exactly the same on the other side. Set legs and breasts aside.

Your next job is to clean the innards out of the carcasses, so take them over to the sink as it is a little more messy. With a sharp knife, slice open the rump of each carcass, near the bone. Pull open to reveal the liver, sitting on top of the rest of the innards. If you are really thrifty, and want to make the most of the birds, cut out the livers and reserve to fry up to make a morsel of pheasant liver pâté, or just to enjoy on toast. Use your fingers to pull out all the innards and throw them out. Now rinse each bird really thoroughly under cold water, working out any remaining bits and bobs and rinsing off the bloody bits. Pull the carcass apart as best you can. If you have time, soak the carcass in salty water to leach out the last of the blood. Gory stuff over and done with.

4

Saturday *supper* in the kitchen for four

Curried Pheasant Chowder

Norah's Baked Pears with **Amaretti Biscuits**

As we arrived at Grange Lodge we crossed paths with Jilly Acheson, who had just delivered a handsome brace of pheasant (she also supplies Norah with old-fashioned dry-cure bacon and ham and other free-range meat). Game, particularly feathered game, is at its best and most prolific in late autumn. If you live in the country you may well be given a brace or two for free – if not now, then in January when the season is drawing to a close. Even if you have to pay, a good game dealer who draws on nearby shoots for his supplies will charge very little for a fine pair of pheasant. If you are prepared to pluck or skin them yourself (much easier than you might imagine), it works out a good deal cheaper than chicken, and tastes far more interesting into the bargain. Venison sells for a good price at this time of year, too, though these days you can get it all year round. Haunch and saddle are the cuts that everyone goes for, which means that much of the rest of the animal is sold off at a more than reasonable price. The cheaper pieces (which may even cost less than equivalent cuts of beef) are ideal for the dark, savoury stews and casseroles that suit the season so well. Add wild field or horse mushrooms, if you can find them and are sure that you have identified them correctly, and you can feed a tableful of hungry people for a snip.

5

Sunday *lunch* for four

Norah's Cheese and **Chutney Purses**

Pan-fried Breasts of **Pheasant** with **Port** and **Elderberry Jelly Gravy**

Loud Mash and **Deep-fried Leek** and **Beetroot Shreds**

Golden Eve's Pudding

Menu 4
Pheasant Stock

You can make this in exactly the same way as chicken stock (see page 154) but I like to give game stock a richer, darker flavour and colour, so I usually brown the pheasant carcasses before adding the other ingredients. Once the browning is done, you can leave the stock to bubble away contentedly on it own, paying it a little attention after an hour or so, when you take out the thighs (no point in wasting good meat ...), and then again after another hour or two when the last of the flavour has been extracted from the bones.

Makes 750 ml–1 litre (1¼–1¾ pints)

the carcasses of 2 pheasants, legs and breasts removed (see page 67), with legs added back in to make the stock
1 tablespoon sunflower or vegetable oil
2 carrots, roughly chopped
1 onion, quartered
1 leek, thickly sliced
3 litres (5¼ pints) water
6 black peppercorns
1 bay leaf
2 sprigs of thyme
2 parsley stems (save the leaves for the chowder)

Break the carcasses up roughly. Heat the oil in a deep saucepan over a high heat. Add the pheasant carcasses and the legs and sizzle and brown on all sides. The browning adds colour and flavour to the stock, so take it as dark as you dare without actually burning it – allow some 10–15 minutes for this. Next add the vegetables and fry for a minute or two more. Pour in the water and add all the remaining ingredients. Bring up to the boil and simmer slowly for 1 hour. Take out the pheasant legs but leave the rest to simmer for a further 1–2 hours to extract every last drop of flavour. While it simmers, pick the meat off the pheasant legs and reserve for the chowder. Toss the bones back into the stockpot. Once the stock is cooked, strain out the bones and vegetables and set aside half the stock for the chowder, half for the gravy for Sunday lunch.

Curried Pheasant Chowder

Chowders are normally made with fish but this one takes the last shreds of meat picked off the bones of the pheasant as its mainstay. Along with that there are chunks of celery, carrot and potato, all bathed in a thick, milky soup, enlivened with a home-made curry powder and finished with a grating of cheese. Filling and satisfying.

If you don't happen to have in your cupboard all the spices listed, you can simplify matters by replacing them with 1½ teaspoons bought mild or medium-hot curry powder.

30 g (1 oz) butter
1 onion, chopped
2 garlic cloves, chopped
2 large carrots, thickly sliced
2 celery stalks, thickly sliced
1 large potato, cut into 2 cm (¾ inch) cubes
1 large parsnip, peeled, cored and cut into cubes
2 tablespoons plain flour
¼ teaspoon each cayenne pepper, ground cumin, ginger, cinnamon and turmeric
½ teaspoon ground coriander
375–450 ml (13–15 fl oz) pheasant stock
600 ml (1 pint) milk
1 bay leaf
1 sprig of thyme
the shredded meat from the pheasant legs
1 tablespoon chopped parsley
salt and pepper
grated mature Cheddar or other good cheese, to serve

Melt the butter in a large pan, then add all the vegetables. Stir around to coat in the butter, then cover and leave to sweat over a low heat for 10–15 minutes, stirring once or twice. Meanwhile, mix the flour with all the spices. Sprinkle the flour mixture over the vegetables, then turn and stir them so that they are evenly coated. Cook for 2 minutes or so, stirring continuously.

Pour in about half of the stock, stir to mix evenly, then add the remaining stock and the milk, as well as the bay leaf, thyme and some salt and pepper. Bring up to the boil, then leave to simmer quietly for about 20 minutes, until the vegetables are all tender. Stir in the shreds of pheasant meat, simmer for another couple of minutes, then adjust the seasoning. Add the parsley, then spoon into generous bowls, sprinkle with cheese and serve immediately, with big hunks of first-class bread.

Norah's Baked Pears with Amaretti Biscuits

Norah rose to the £5 challenge magnificently. As if her fabulous home-baked breads (see pages 77–9) weren't enough, she then produced this pudding of pears (10 pence each in Dungannon market) baked with a filling of crushed amaretti biscuits, gingernuts and dried apricots, the whole served with a drizzle of purple damson sauce (see page 80), which she had made earlier in the season when damsons were free for the taking in the hedgerows.

85 g (3 oz) gingernut biscuits	
75 g (2½ oz) amaretti biscuits	
45 g (1½ oz) butter, melted	
45 g (1½ oz) dried apricots, finely chopped	
a pinch of cinnamon	
30 g (1 oz) light demerara sugar	
2 tablespoons condensed milk	
4 medium-sized firm conference pears	
juice of ½–1 lemon	
125 ml (4 fl oz) Damson Sauce (see page 80)	
a little single cream, to serve	

Pre-heat the oven to 200°C/400°F/Gas Mark 6.

Put the gingernuts and amaretti into a polythene bag and crush with a rolling pin. Use a little of the melted butter to grease a shallow ovenproof dish, just large enough to hold 8 pear halves in a single layer.

Put the crushed biscuits, chopped apricots, cinnamon and sugar into a bowl and add the remaining butter and the condensed milk. Mix well until all the ingredients hold together.

Peel the pears, cut them in half lengthways and turn in the lemon juice to prevent browning. Fill each pear half with the biscuit mixture, covering most of the exposed area. Place in the buttered dish and bake for 15–20 minutes.

Thin the damson sauce with a little water if necessary, to the consistency of single cream. Remove the baked pears from the oven and serve with the sauce and a touch of single cream.

Menu 5
Norah's Cheese and Chutney Purses

Norah snapped up a jar of the spiced carrot and garlic chutney I'd made and declared that she had a grand idea for it. While I sat peeling apples for the pudding, she quickly made up a foursome of plump, luscious-looking filo pastry purses, stuffed to the gills with the chutney and plenty of grated Ulster Cheddar mixed with lightly sautéed spring onions. A neat idea, especially as the purses can be made a few hours in advance, to be popped into the oven quarter of an hour or so before eating.

Of course, any good-quality mature Cheddar can be used for these parcels or, indeed, any other good melting cheese with a pronounced flavour. If you don't just happen to have a cache of carrot and garlic chutney in the cupboard, then any good-quality, sweet, sharp and spicy chutney can replace it.

30 g (1 oz) butter, melted

1 large spring onion, chopped

110 g (4 oz) Cheddar cheese, grated

1 tablespoon chopped parsley

4 large sheets of filo pastry

4 generous teaspoons Spiced Carrot and Garlic Chutney (see page 81)

freshly ground black pepper

To serve

a few rocket leaves or sprigs of parsley

4 cherry tomatoes, halved

Pre-heat the oven to 200°C/400°F/Gas Mark 6, unless you are making the filo purses in advance, in which case pre-heat shortly before cooking the purses.

Heat a small frying pan and brush with a little of the melted butter. Sauté the spring onion lightly in the butter. Remove from the heat and mix with the cheese, a good sprinkling of black pepper and the parsley. Divide the mixture into 4 and roll into balls.

Take the 4 sheets of filo out of the packet and cover with a sheet of greaseproof paper and over that a tea towel wrung out in cold water, to prevent them drying out. Take the first sheet and brush lightly with melted butter. Fold in half and then in half again to form, more or less, a square. Brush each side with melted butter, place a teaspoon of chutney in the centre of the filo, then top with a cheese ball. Gather the 4 corners up and squeeze together like a string purse. Repeat with the remaining filo and filling to make 4 purses. Brush the tops with any left-over butter and place the purses on a greased baking sheet. They can be made to this point up to 4 hours in advance, then kept in the fridge until ready to cook.

Cover the upper part of each purse with a little square of silver foil to prevent burning. Bake for 15 minutes, removing the foil after 10 minutes so that the tops can brown. Remove from the oven and serve with a few rocket leaves or parsley sprigs and the cherry tomatoes.

Pan-Fried Breasts of Pheasant with Port and Elderberry Jelly Gravy

Pheasant breasts are very quick to cook – a few minutes in the frying pan is all it takes and, with the aid of a measure of intense, reduced pheasant stock, a slug of port or whatever other sweet fortified wine you care to use, and a little fruit jelly, you can knock up a superb gravy while the meat is resting.

The two optional extras, both of which I can heartily recommend, are the neon-pink beetroot mash and the crisp shreds of deep-fried leek and beetroot (see page 73), which add an extra note of crispness.

2 tablespoons sunflower oil

2 tablespoons port, sweet Marsala or Madeira, or sweet sherry

1 tablespoon sherry vinegar or red wine vinegar

1 garlic clove, crushed

4 skinned pheasant breasts (see page 67)

375–450 ml (13–15 fl oz) pheasant stock (see page 70)

15 g (½ oz) unsalted butter

1 tablespoon Elderberry Jelly (see page 80), or bramble or redcurrant jelly

salt and pepper

Mix together 1 tablespoon of the oil, the port or other fortified wine, vinegar, garlic and salt and pepper. Marinate the pheasant breasts in this mixture for at least 30 minutes (24 hours is better). Meanwhile, pour the stock into a wide pan and boil down until reduced by half. Remove from the heat and reserve.

When you are nearly ready to eat, take the pheasant breasts out of the marinade and pat dry. Strain the marinade. Heat the remaining tablespoon of oil with the butter in a frying pan large enough to take all 4 breasts.

When the oil and butter are foaming, add the pheasant breasts and fry over a moderate heat for 4–5 minutes on each side, until just cooked through. Transfer them to a warm serving dish and leave to rest in a warm place while you finish the gravy.

Tip out any excess fat from the frying pan, then return the pan to the heat. Pour in the strained marinade and bring up to the boil, stirring and scraping in any residues from frying the pheasant, then pour in the reduced stock. Bring up to the boil, then stir in the jelly until melted, and finally season to taste. If the gravy is getting too sparse and boiled down, add a splash of hot water to dilute.

To serve, place a pheasant breast on top of a mound of Loud Mash (see below) on each plate. Spoon over some of the gravy and top with a tangle of deep-fried leek and beetroot (see page 76).

Loud Mash

As I served the main course of our lunch, the eyes of Norah's daughter, Jennifer, widened at the vivid pink of the mashed potatoes. 'That is the loudest mash I've ever seen,' she said, and it's true. The colour of mashed potato is never going to get any louder than this. It tastes pretty good, too, and is the best way I know of getting children to eat beetroot. The colour of the cooked, grated beetroot bleeds into the pale mashed potatoes, turning them a glorious, bright pink. Very eye-catching.

Make the mash in advance by all means, but don't stir in the beetroot until the last minute or it will discolour. The beetroot can be boiled but I prefer to bake them, wrapped individually in silver foil, in a low to moderate oven (the exact temperature doesn't matter that much) for several hours, until the skin scrapes away easily from the stalk end.

around 340 g (12 oz) cooked beetroot, peeled
600 g (1 lb 5 oz) floury potatoes, boiled until tender, then peeled
30 g (1 oz) butter
150–300 ml (¼–½ pint) creamy milk
salt, pepper and nutmeg

Grate the cooked beetroot (use a food processor if possible – it makes for a far less messy undertaking). Mash the potatoes in the pan while still warm, with the butter and seasoning. Place over a moderate heat and gradually whisk in enough milk to form a soft, creamy mash. If necessary, reheat the potatoes just before serving. Stir in the beetroot, taste and adjust the seasoning.

Deep-fried Leek and Beetroot Shreds

This is just a bit of fun, the kind of thing you get in restaurants to add some height to a dish and, more importantly for the domestic cook, a contrasting texture in the form of a crisp crunch. I wouldn't suggest fiddling about with strips of leek and beetroot for a weekday supper but this, after all, is Sunday lunch, the one day in the week when you should have time to go to town.

Have a practice run first. The trick to this sort of thing is getting the heat of the oil just right, hot enough to crisp and brown without actually burning. Speed, concentration and good judgement also play a crucial part; this is not something to turn your hand to if there is any form of major distraction – howling baby, squabbling children, impatient partner, or whatever – since for a few minutes you will have to give it your full attention.

A word of warning about leeks. If you want your leek to curl and corkscrew prettily you must use a

continued on page 76

continued from page 73

young, relatively slender one. When we were filming in Northern Ireland we were all mightily perplexed when our finely shredded leeks flatly and stiffly refused to curve after seemingly endless hours of soaking in iced water. When we finally discarded the first two batches, cut from stonking big mature leeks, and tried yet again with a new batch of younger, thinner specimens, we found they did curl precisely as they should after a couple of hours. ·

1 leek, trimmed and thoroughly cleaned
½ medium-to-large raw beetroot, peeled
juice of ½ lemon
oil for deep-frying

Cut the leek into 7.5–10 cm (3–4 inch) lengths, then halve each piece lengthways and cut into long, fine threads. Drop into a bowl of iced water, add a few ice cubes and leave in the fridge for at least 2 hours to curl the strands. Grate the beetroot coarsely, using long strokes (for once a manual grater is preferable) to get the longest possible beetroot threads. Mix with the lemon juice, then cover and reserve until needed.

Shortly before eating, drain the leek and beetroot separately, then dry thoroughly on kitchen paper. Heat a medium pan of oil or an electric deep-fat fryer to about 180°C/350°F, or when a cube of bread fizzles vigorously as it is dropped in and browns within 20–30 seconds. Drop in small handfuls of the leek (be careful, as the oil bubbles up in a more than lively fashion at first) and deep-fry for 40–90 seconds, until golden brown but no more, then scoop out swiftly and drain on kitchen paper. If the first batch is verging on black, lower the heat under the oil, wait a few minutes and try again. Once all the leek has been fried, fry the beetroot in the same way but make the timing shorter – some 25–40 seconds should be enough. Lift out before you lose all the dark red colour, then drain on kitchen paper. Serve a tangle of fried mixed shreds on top of each helping of pheasant.

Golden Eve's Pudding

Eve's pudding is one of those comforting, old-fashioned, utterly delicious autumn puddings, with a layer of soft apple at the bottom and a light sponge baked over the top. Well, this version hangs on to all that is good about the original but brings it bang up to date by replacing some of the flour with sunshine-yellow polenta (use the quick-cooking sort that most good supermarkets and Italian delis sell) and adding a clean dash of lemon. The polenta gives the topping a slightly grainy texture and a glossy golden crumb which is wonderfully appealing against the tender apple. An ideal pudding for any family lunch or supper.

If you make the apple base in advance, be sure to heat it up thoroughly before pouring it into the dish and covering with the polenta topping. You need that burst of heat from underneath to cook the golden sponge properly. If you pour it on to cold apple, you'll end up with a well-browned top and a runny batter underneath.

650 g (1½ lb) cooking apples, peeled, cored and chopped
1 tablespoon honey
finely grated zest of ½ lemon
30 g (1 oz) caster sugar

For the topping
60 g (2 oz) polenta
30 g (1 oz) plain flour
1 teaspoon baking powder
60 g (2 oz) caster sugar
a pinch of salt
finely grated zest of ½ lemon
1 egg, lightly beaten
60 g (2 oz) melted butter, cooled until tepid
juice of ½ lemon
a little milk (1–2 tablespoons)

Pre-heat the oven to 200°C/400°F/Gas Mark 6.

Put the apples into a pan with the honey, lemon zest and sugar. Cover and cook over a medium heat until the juice has begun to run – a mere 3–5 minutes should do it. Uncover and continue cooking until a fair proportion of the apples has collapsed to a purée but a few chunks remain intact (a further 10–15 minutes). Stir well, then tip into a 1.5 litre (2½ pint) pie dish and spread out.

To make the topping, mix all the dry ingredients, including the lemon zest, together in a bowl and make a well in the centre. Pour in the egg, melted butter and lemon juice and mix well, gradually bringing in the other ingredients. Add enough milk to give a loose dropping consistency. Dollop the mixture over the cooked apples, then carefully spread it out smoothly and evenly to cover them.

Bake for about 25–30 minutes, until the topping is firm to the touch and pulling away from the edges of the dish. Serve hot or warm, with single or double cream if the budget will stretch to it.

6

Norah's *Breads*

Soda Farls

Treacle and **Sultana Soda Bannock**

Ireland produces many superb foodstuffs, none better than its bread. The average high-street baker there makes bread that puts most mainland shops to shame, but it gets even better in the homes of good Irish cooks like Norah, who make their own. For breakfast we ate toasted treacle and sultana bread, and with our chowder at supper we devoured brown and white soda farls, all freshly baked every day, all with substance and individual character.

I asked Norah for her bread-making secrets. 'Och, that's easy, Sophie,' she replied. And it is, if you live in Ireland and have a will to bake. There are no tricks or clever twists. What it comes down to is the flour and the buttermilk. The quality of the flour is outstanding, especially the brown flour with its nutty flavour, but more than that, Norah can buy ready-mixed bags of flour, bicarbonate of soda, cream of tartar and salt in any grocery store, big or small.

Previous double page (From left to right): Treacle and Sultana Soda Bannock; Soda Farls

The proportions are perfect, and the mechanical mixing ensures that the added ingredients are evenly distributed through the flour. The buttermilk, which is just as easy to find, is real buttermilk or, in other words, the liquid left over after making butter. What I can buy on the mainland is cultured buttermilk, with something of the taste of the real thing but made in the same fashion as yoghurt.

Still, Norah relented and gave me some tips on making something akin to proper Irish bread with the less than perfect ingredients I have to hand at home. Since returning from Ireland I've tried some of the ready-made soda or scofa bread mixes and found them surprisingly good, though Norah's adapted recipes are even better.

Soda Farls

Cut a disc of bread dough into quarters and you end up with four 'farls'. The word comes originally from Scotland, where quarter-circle oatcakes and shortbread are also known as farls. Irish soda farls are made with either white or brown flour, raised with bicarbonate of soda and cream of tartar. You will need either a heavy, flat-based frying pan or a flat griddle pan to cook them on, but with that in hand they are probably the quickest and easiest of breads to make. They look tremendous, and taste very good indeed.

Serve them still slightly warm from the griddle if you can. Failing that they will keep for a day or two in an airtight tin. Split them in half and spread with butter to enjoy with soups and main courses, or toast them and serve with butter and jam for breakfast or tea.

300 g (10 oz) plain white flour, strong white bread flour or wholemeal flour
1 level teaspoon bicarbonate of soda
1 level teaspoon cream of tartar
¾ teaspoon salt
250–300 ml (8–10 fl oz) buttermilk

Put the flour into a large mixing bowl, add the bicarbonate of soda, cream of tartar and salt and mix together. Make a well in the centre and add the buttermilk. Mix to a stiff dough with a wooden spoon. Turn out on to a lightly floured work surface and knead gently to form a smooth round. Roll out into a circle about 20 cm (8 inches) in diameter and no more than 1 cm (½ inch) thick. Cut into farls, i.e. quarters.

Put a flat griddle or a cast-iron frying pan over a medium heat. Do not grease. To test the pan, sprinkle a little flour over the surface. When it begins to turn golden brown, the heat is right. Sprinkle more flour lightly over the surface of the griddle to prevent sticking and then lay the farls on it. Cook for 6–8 minutes on each side, until light beige in colour and hollow-sounding when tapped. You can see the dough rising as it cooks – fascinating. Once the farls are done, wrap in a clean cloth and allow to cool before using.

Treacle and Sultana Soda Bannock

This became an essential part of my breakfasts while I was staying with Norah. The basic mixture is much the same as that used for soda farls but the black treacle and plump sultanas change it completely. I love it fresh, lightly buttered for tea, or with cheese and a salad at lunchtime, but I like it even better toasted and slathered with salty butter first thing in the morning.

450 g (1 lb) wholemeal flour
1 heaped teaspoon bicarbonate of soda
1 heaped teaspoon cream of tartar
1 teaspoon salt
30 g (1 oz) butter, diced
200 g (7 oz) sultanas
3 tablespoons black treacle or molasses
425–475 ml (14–16 fl oz) buttermilk

Pre-heat the oven to 200°C/400°F/Gas Mark 6.

Grease either a 17.5 cm (7 inch) round cake tin, 6 cm (2¼ inches) deep, or a 900 g (2 lb) loaf tin. Mix the flour with the bicarbonate of soda, cream of tartar and salt in a large bowl. Rub in the butter, then stir in the sultanas. Make a well in the centre and add the treacle or molasses and the buttermilk. Mix to form a soft dough.

Either shape into a round and place in the cake tin or form into a longer roll and lay in the loaf tin. Sprinkle the top with a little flour. Bake for 30 minutes, then reduce the heat to 150°C/300°F/Gas Mark 2 and bake for a further 30 minutes, until the bread sounds hollow when tapped on the bottom. Turn out and cool on a wire rack.

7

Stashing Away the *Harvest*

Elderberry Jelly

Damson Sauce for the **Freezer**

Spiced Carrot and **Garlic Chutney**

There always comes a day when you sniff that first sniff of autumn in the air, when you know that the year has turned, that the season of growth has reached its peak, and that over the next few months the greens of summer will soften to the golds and reds and browns of autumn. As the year begins to wane, there's one last glorious spurt of activity in the plant world, and one last burst of fruit and vegetables to gather in. Autumn sees its own gluts of vegetables and fruits, and some of the best are wild and free for the picking.

If I have plenty of time, then I make a point of going blackberrying, before 10 October, which is when, legend has it, the Devil casts his evil over all the blackberry bushes, blighting the fruit (in many parts of the country it is about the time the first frosts strike). If the year is good, I make up a stock of blackberry jelly (simmer 1 kilo (2 lbs) blackberries with the juice of a lemon and 300 ml (½ pint) water for an hour, strain as for elderberry jelly, then for every 600 ml (1 pint) juice, weigh out 450g (1 lb) granulated sugar, and continue as for elderberry jelly, page 80). However, elderberry jam has to be my all-time favourite. Elderberries are everywhere, with their strong and distinctive taste, that needs to be tamed gently with the help of a few cooking apples, also now in the height of their season. Then their are tart damsons, the last of the years plums, which are magnificent in crumbles and pies. These small, beautiful plums often grow in hedgerows, as well as in gardens, but even if you have to buy them, they are never prohibitively expensive.

Making autumn preserves is not something that can be done in an instant, or even in half an hour, but at the weekend, a stroll down green lanes with friends or the family to gather what is freely on offer, or a session round the kitchen table together as you   pick over and prepare the fruit or vegetables for cooking, can be just as much fun as heading straight to the pub, and a darn sight less costly. The results of your travails will definitely be appreciated, and will taste so much better than shop bought jellies, jams and chutneys. What's more they make excellent gifts, if you can bear to part with them.

Elderberry Jelly

Early autumn finds Norah out raiding the hedgerows around and about her house. She picks damsons to make damson sauce (see below) and elderberries to make this superb, slightly tart, dark-purple jelly. It goes particularly well with game but is good, too, with lamb or cold ham. Pot it in small jam jars, since it is quite strong and you will only use a little at a time.

Makes about 2.25–2.75 kg (5–6 lb)

650 g (1½ lb) elderberries
650 g (1½ lb) cooking apples
granulated sugar

Pick over the elderberries to remove stray leaves and insects and other unwanted bits and bobs but don't even consider stripping them off their stalks – there's really no need. Place in a large preserving pan. Cut any bruised or damages patches out of the apples, then cut them up into chunks, skin,

core and all, and add to the elderberries. Pour in enough water to almost cover the fruit. Bring up to the boil and simmer for 1 hour, until the fruit is very soft and squishy. Spoon the fruit into a jelly bag suspended over a large bowl so that the juices can drip down into it (if you don't have a jelly bag you can improvise with a J-cloth, rinsed thoroughly in boiling water, then used to line a large non-metallic sieve set over a large bowl). Leave for at least 8 hours or overnight, and don't be tempted to press down on the fruit to speed up the process – if you do you will end up with cloudy jelly.

Chuck out the debris in the jelly bag and measure the juice. Weigh out 340 g (12 oz) sugar for every 600 ml (1 pint) of juice. Put the juice and sugar into a pan and stir over a moderate heat until the sugar has completely dissolved. Bring up to the boil and boil hard until setting point is reached (see page 124) – around 10 minutes. Skim off any scum and pour the jelly into hot, sterilized jars (see page 124). Cover and seal, then label and store in a cool, dark, dry cupboard.

Damson Sauce for the Freezer

Norah has inspired me to make more use of the damsons that grow in the fields around our house. Every year she picks basketfuls of these astringent, purple-black plums with their remarkable aroma. Some she transforms into jelly but when time is at a premium she simple cooks them to a pulp, sweetens it and then pops it in the freezer, ready to use at a moment's notice. Thinned down with a little water, it makes a superb sauce for late autumn and winter puddings – try it with her baked pears on page 71 – or just drizzled over ice-cream.

For every 1 kg (2¼ lb) damsons

300 ml (½ pint) water
icing or caster sugar to taste

Weigh the damsons and calculate how much water you will need. Put the damsons into a pan with the water and bring up to the boil. Reduce the heat, cover and simmer for about 20 minutes, until the damsons are very soft. Peer into the pan once in a while and lift out with a slotted spoon any stones that have risen to the surface.

Place a large nylon sieve (the acidity of the damsons could react with a metal one) over a capacious bowl and tip in the contents of the saucepan. Rub the pulp of the fruit through the sieve into the bowl. Stir in sugar to taste. Leave to cool, then freeze in small pots to use whenever needed.

Spiced Carrot and Garlic Chutney

Smart spicy chutneys are on the increase, and you can shell out a small fortune for them in delis, gift shops and even supermarkets these days. However, if you relish something a little bit different and a big bit special to savour with a slice of good ham or cheese, then you'll be delighted to find that it doesn't take much knowhow, or much money, to conjure it up at home. I'll bet you'd find it hard to buy many chutneys that taste anywhere near as good as this one, and certainly not at well under £4 for ten jars.

Prepare the carrots the day before you want to cook the chutney, so that the salt and vinegar have time to draw out their moisture as they sit overnight. I like to leave the whole spices in the chutney but

if you don't fancy biting into a chunk of star anise, then parcel all the spices up in a square of butter muslin (available from most half-way decent fabric shops, or from cookware shops, though it will be more expensive), tied with a long piece of string. Pop the bag in the preserving pan with all the other ingredients and tie the string to the handle, so that the bag can be located and pulled out easily and quickly.

Makes ten 450 g (1 lb) jars

1.8 kg (4 lb) carrots, coarsely grated
110 g (4 oz) fresh root ginger, peeled and finely chopped
1 litre (1¾ pints) cider vinegar
8 dried red chillies
2 tablespoons coarsely crushed coriander seeds
4 cinnamon sticks
2 star anise
60 g (2 oz) coarse sea salt
3 heads of garlic
500 ml (17 fl oz) water
1.5 kg (3 lb) granulated sugar

Put the carrots in a bowl with the ginger, cider vinegar, chillies, spices and salt. Mix together, cover with a tea towel and then leave for 24 hours, or at least overnight.

Next day, separate the heads of garlic into individual cloves and peel them all. Scrape and pour the carrot mixture into a large preserving pan and add the garlic and water. Bring up to the boil and simmer for 10 minutes, then stir in the sugar. Bring back up to the boil, and then boil hard for about 45 minutes, stirring occasionally, until the chutney is thick and jammy. Let it settle off the heat for about 3 minutes, then while it is still good and hot ladle it into hot, sterilized jars (see page 124) and seal tightly with non-corrosive lids. Label and then store in a cool, dry, dark place. It tastes pretty good as soon as it has been made, but even better if you wait for a week or more before dipping in.

8

The comfort zone – *warming food* for four

Rosemary and **Garlic Lamb Chops** on **Garlicky Chickpea Mash** with **Garlic Jam**

Compote of **Apples** and **Raisins** with **Nutmeg** and **Greek Yoghurt**

Previous page
(From left to right):
Rosemary and Garlic
Lamb Chops on Garlicky
Chickpea Mash with
Garlic Jam; Compote of
Apples and Raisins
with Nutmeg and
Greek Yoghurt

There's a distinctly comfortable, familiar feel to this menu – chops and mash, stewed apple – old-fashioned, plain cooking. But wait a minute ... all is not as it seems at first glance. We're still slap-bang in the middle of the comfort zone here but, far from being old-fashioned, this food is right up there with the latest trends. Take the mash, for a start: it's a chickpea mash, enlivened with oodles of garlic, the kind of thing that appears in smart London bistros and costs them next to nothing, though they charge plenty for it. The lamb chops, too, are laden with garlic, but plainly grilled and accompanied by a tremendous relish of candied garlic spiked with chilli and rosemary. Stewed apples have never tasted so good, cooked slowly with plump, succulent raisins until almost candied, and finished with a scraping of nutmeg and a dollop of rich Greek yoghurt. Not at all like Granny used to make ... So put your chickpeas to soak and get ready to step right into the modern comfort zone.

Rosemary and Garlic Lamb Chops on Garlicky Chickpea Mash with Garlic Jam

Chickpea mash has become a very trendy accompaniment of late and it is easy to see why. It is cheap to make, especially if you use dried chickpeas, and very easy too, as long as you remember to soak the chickpeas overnight. The finished tawny mash can be made gorgeously garlicky, with a slight lick of lemon in it to take the edge off the leguminous quality of chickpeas. It goes especially well with lamb, and then to finish the combination off with a flourish there's a surprisingly delicious garlic jam.

If you have any mash left over it reheats well, and is rather good served with shavings of Parmesan and a knob of butter as a starter.

4 small lamb chops
leaves of 1 small sprig of rosemary
a little olive oil
salt and pepper

For the mash

225 g (8 oz) dried chickpeas, soaked overnight
3 tablespoons olive oil
juice of ½–1 lemon

For the garlic jam

1 large head of garlic
60 g (2 oz) granulated or caster sugar
125 ml (4 fl oz) water
1 small sprig of rosemary
1 dried red chilli

Take the head of garlic for the garlic jam and separate into individual cloves. Peel the whole lot of them. Cut one clove up into long, thin needles for the chops. Slice 3 of them for the mash and leave the rest whole for the jam.

Make slits in the lamb chops and push in the slivers of garlic and the rosemary leaves. Season with pepper only. Cover and set aside until needed.

For the mash, drain the chickpeas and put into a pan with enough water to cover generously. Do not add any salt. Bring up to the boil, boil hard for 5 minutes, then reduce the heat and simmer gently until tender – this will take 1–2 hours, depending on the age and size of the chickpeas. Drain the chickpeas, reserving about 300 ml (½ pint) of their cooking liquid. Place them in a food processor with the sliced garlic, olive oil, salt and pepper and the juice of half a lemon. Process to a mash, gradually drizzling in enough of the cooking water to give a smooth but soft purée that is almost, but not quite, runny – you may not need all the reserved liquid. Taste and adjust the seasoning, adding more lemon juice if needed. Transfer to a pan and warm through gently, if necessary, while the lamb chops are cooking.

While the chickpeas are simmering, make the garlic jam. Drop the whole garlic cloves into a small pan of boiling water, bring back to the boil, simmer for 2 minutes, then drain. Put the sugar, water, rosemary and chilli in a saucepan and stir over a low heat until the sugar has completely dissolved.

Now add the blanched garlic and simmer gently for about 40 minutes until the cloves are translucent and completely tender. Tip into a small bowl with the cooking syrup and leave to cool.

Pre-heat the grill thoroughly. Brush the lamb chops lightly with oil and grill close to the heat for about 3 minutes on each side (or a little longer if you like them well done). Season with salt. Divide the mash between 4 warmed plates and lay a lamb chop on top of each. Spoon some of the garlic jam on to each plate and serve.

Compote of Apples and Raisins with Nutmeg and Greek Yoghurt

This compote of apples and raisins is one that we make in copious quantities every year when the apples ripen in our garden. We eat it for pudding (the children love it) and for breakfast, and it can be used as a pie or tart filling as well, if the fancy takes you. It can be made several days in advance, and served warm or cold. The mild creamy tartness of Greek yoghurt balances the sweetness.

110 g (4 oz) caster sugar
85 g (3 oz) light muscovado sugar
450 ml (¾ pint) water
500 g (1 lb 2 oz) good eating apples (more or less – don't waste half an apple to get the exact quantity), peeled, cored and cut into eighths
60 g (2 oz) raisins
freshly grated nutmeg
4 tablespoons Greek yoghurt, to serve

Put the two sugars into a pan with the water and stir over a moderate heat until completely dissolved. Bring up to the boil. Add the apples and raisins, and a scraping of fresh nutmeg. Simmer very gently for about 30 minutes, until the apple slices are translucent and very tender. Scoop them out into a shallow dish or bowl with a slotted spoon and add another fresh rasping of nutmeg. Boil the juice down for 3 or 4 minutes, until syrupy, then pour it over the apples. Serve warm or cold, with the Greek yoghurt.

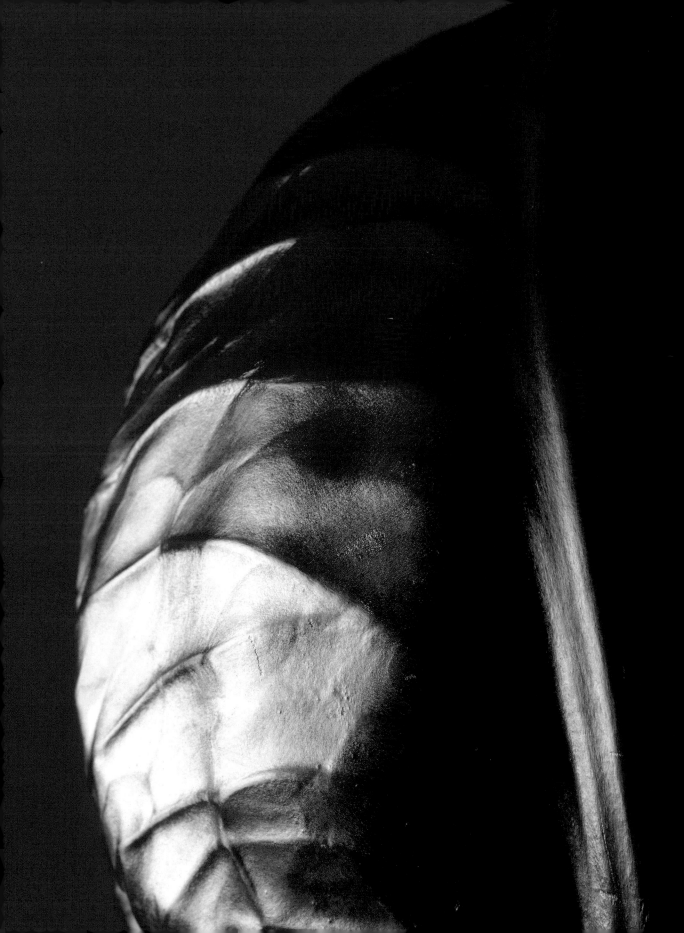

Twenty-four Hours in *Exotic* Leicester

Imagine a cross between 'Friends', 'This Life' and 'Men Behaving Badly'. Transpose it to Leicester for a somewhat grittier feel, then think about a few good careers for our house-sharers: what about, for instance, throwing together a graphic designer, a DJ who also happens to be a chef, a marketing manager for a local newspaper, the manager of a snazzy upmarket clothes shop, and a careworker for people with learning disabilities?

What do you get (apart from some good storylines)? Well, I'll tell you what you get: you get Paul, Neil, Louise, Rory and Craig, and not a television creation amongst them. All real-life flesh and blood, and having a ball sharing a house together. This group has been together for over three years now, and they've known each other for much longer. It's quite obvious within minutes of sitting down in their living room with them that they are all great friends, with a shared history of wild parties and tall stories and mad escapades. What makes this close proximity work for them is that they all lead independent lives away from the house they share.

Very soon it is apparent that they also share a love of good food (and drink, but perhaps I'd better keep quiet about that, except to say that you can still see the damage inflicted on the living-room door by the vodka jelly ...), which is where I come into the picture. My task for the day was to create a sumptuous birthday banquet for Louise, while the boys turned the living room into a candlelit maharajah's dining room.

Leicester is less than an hour's drive from where I live, and for ages I'd been meaning to visit it. Finally this quintet of friends had provided me with the perfect excuse to go and explore Leicester's famous market (the largest covered market in Europe, they claim) and, perhaps even more alluring, its legendary 'golden mile', the length of Belgrave Road that is at the heart of the city's Asian community. For all Louise, Craig, Neil, Paul and Rory's cosmopolitan tastes in food, I discovered that they made relatively little use of the wealth of Asian food stores in the city, and that they steered clear of the more unusual herbs and spices on the market. That did it. The banquet's theme was instantly clear – East meets West or, to be more precise, India meets Europe. Just as I had hoped, the rainy streets of Leicester came up trumps, with marvellous ingredients at bin-end prices. Neil led me off to the golden mile and, as we strolled past shops selling saris in all the colours of the rainbow, jeweller's heaving with intricate Indian gold necklaces and earrings, food stores boasting racks of spices and big, verdant bunches of coriander, mint and methi (fenugreek), and fascinating sweetmeat shops and restaurants, he soon caught my enthusiasm for the theme I'd chosen. He redesigned the birthday cake he was planning (page 103) and dived suddenly into a spruce Asian sweet and savoury snack shop, the wonderful Sharmilee's, to make secret purchases. All was to be revealed later that evening when the grand banquet was finally unveiled ...

The deal was clear enough. I cooked the birthday banquet, Neil showed me around Leicester, helped me to shop and took charge of the cake, while Paul and Rory put heart and soul into dressing up the living room. Meanwhile, Craig was taking birthday girl Louise shopping all day, at her request. Neil's enthusiasm for the fusing of India and Europe gathered speed, and before the rest of us knew it lunch was produced to stoke us

1

A light, bright *lunch* for four

Brightside Baked Potatoes

up for the task ahead. One course only – after all he didn't want to take us away from our allotted tasks for too long – but enough to set the scene for the evening's bash. With the potatoes, Neil served a salad of watercress and orange, lightly dressed with wine vinegar, olive oil, salt and pepper.

Brightside Baked Potatoes

Emblazoned above the door to their house is the word 'Brightside', a singularly incongruous name for a house with a view over vast metal air-conditioning units from the factory next door to a busy arterial road. It fits this brightly coloured dish of baked potatoes topped with spiced chicken and red peppers far better.

4 baking potatoes
6 tablespoons natural yoghurt
salt and pepper

For the filling
2 chicken breasts, diced
½ teaspoon ground turmeric
1 teaspoon ground coriander
1 garlic clove, crushed
1 onion, diced
1 teaspoon olive oil
1 tablespoon sunflower or olive oil
1 red pepper, deseeded and diced
4 tablespoons roughly chopped fresh coriander

Pre-heat the oven to 200°C/400°F/Gas Mark 6.

Prick the skins of the potatoes all over with a fork to prevent bursting. Dampen the skins lightly, then rub with salt. Place on a baking tray and bake for about 1 hour, until tender all the way through. Season the yoghurt lightly with salt and pepper.

Meanwhile, mix the chicken with the turmeric, ground coriander, garlic, onion, olive oil and some salt and pepper and leave for half an hour, until the potatoes are just about cooked. Heat the sunflower or olive oil in a frying pan and sauté the chicken mixture for 2 minutes over a medium heat. Add the diced pepper and continue sautéing until the chicken is cooked through and the pepper is tender. Draw off the heat and stir in the coriander. Cut a deep cross in the top of each potato, taking it about two thirds of the way down towards the base. Using thumb and index finger of both hands, placed evenly between the cuts, squeeze the base of each potato firmly, until the top opens to reveal the white flesh inside, like the 4 petals of a flower. Spoon the chicken mixture into the 4 steaming potatoes, then top each one with 1½ tablespoons of yoghurt. Serve immediately.

East-meets-West birthday *banquet* for six

Onion and **Almond Bhajis** with **Agro Dolce Date Sauce**

Seared Spiced Salmon Fillet with **Herb Butter**

Masala Mushy Peas

Roast Roots and **Alliums** with **Tamarind**

Stir-fried Spinach with **Cashew Nuts, Currants** and **South Indian Spices**

Mint, Grape and **Cucumber Raita**

Onion Cachumber

This is the mega-luxury meal of the book. Not a mere £5 for a whole meal. Nothing as niggardly as that. Oh no. Just for once, I've flung caution to the winds and I'm going for broke. For one night only, it's a whole fiver per head! That's a cool £30 to spend in all. Let me admit now that I had trouble spending it all. There is enough food here to feed an army – perhaps I exaggerate, but certainly more than enough for six people and even enough for eight as long as you add a couple more pieces of salmon and share the naans, or make a couple extra – and the grand total came to around £26.

When it came to conjuring it all up *in situ* in Leicester, time got the better of me, and I had to leave out one dish, the Masala Mushy Peas. No one noticed, no one complained. I'm still including the recipe here, because it is so good and easy, and provides a wetter, more-liquid addition to moisten the rice. Anyway, the upshot was that this knocked even more off the bill, bringing it down to around £25. What to do with the extra fiver? The best solution I could come up with was to invest in some edible silver leaf to decorate the pudding, which only set me back another two quid. In the end I gave up, and put the last of the change into the kitty for drink.

If you don't fancy recreating the entire banquet, you will find that the individual dishes can be mixed and matched with other foods quite happily. There is only one expensive dish amongst them and that is the salmon. You can't cook that for less than a fiver, but for a special occasion it really is worth splashing out on it. The rest are all low-cost but high on flavour. Make one or two alone for a simple supper and you won't be disappointed.

Naan Bread with **Coriander Pesto**

Cardamom Coconut Jelly with **Vark**

Mango and **Lime Kulfi**

Poached Starfruit

Onion and Almond Bhajis

One of the great joys of Indian cooking is all the marvellous little savoury snacks, the samosas, bhajis, pakoras and so on, that we've appropriated over here to form first courses for Indian meals. These bhajis are more than just plain onion flavour – they also contain carrot for sweetness, potato for texture, lentils for their nutty crunch and flaked almonds as well. They are held together with gram flour, which is made of finely ground dried chickpeas and can be bought in Asian food stores, as well as in some Italian delicatessens, where it will be called *farina di ceci*, though it will probably be more expensive there.

Of course, all these snacks are best eaten as soon as they have been cooked, but if you want to get ahead, well before everyone sits down ravenous to eat, make the mixture and deep-fry the bhajis until they are three-quarters cooked, then finish them off in hot oil just before eating. If you really can't take the thought of two sessions of deep-frying, then cook the bhajis fully and reheat them in a hot oven to crisp them up – the results are not quite so good, but acceptable. The one thing to avoid like the plague is reheating them in the microwave, which is the ruination of many an Indian snack, making them tough and rubbery.

Serve the piping-hot, crisp, savoury onion and almond bhajis with the sweet-sour date sauce opposite.

Makes about 30

60 g (2 oz) green lentils
2 large onions, very thinly sliced
1 large carrot, grated
1½ teaspoons salt
150 g (5 oz) gram (chickpea) flour
¼ teaspoon baking powder
1 teaspoon ground turmeric
1 teaspoon ground coriander
2 teaspoons cumin seeds
1 medium potato, peeled and grated
3 tablespoons chopped fresh coriander
30 g (1 oz) flaked almonds
sunflower or vegetable oil for deep-frying

Soak the lentils in water for 4 hours. Spread the onions and carrot out in a colander and sprinkle with the salt. Leave for 30 minutes, then squeeze out any excess moisture. Drain the lentils and dry on kitchen paper. Sift the flour with the baking powder and ground spices. Mix in all the ingredients, except the oil, thoroughly, using your hands.

Heat a large pan of oil to 175°C/340°F, or until a cube of bread dropped into it fizzles gently. Scoop up dessertspoonfuls of the mixture, roll them into balls and drop them into the oil. Do not overcrowd the pan – fry no more than 6 or 7 at a time. If you are serving the bhajis immediately, cook them until richly browned – this should take around 7 minutes. If you are going to reheat them later, cook until just golden brown. Drain on kitchen paper, then serve immediately, if not reheating, with the date sauce. To reheat, heat the oil again to 190°C/375°F and return the bhajis to it for a few minutes until well browned. Drain again on kitchen paper and serve immediately while they are still crisp and hot.

Agro Dolce Date Sauce

Date sauce is a common accompaniment to Indian deep-fried snacks, and very good it is, too. This version brings it slightly nearer to home, with a touch of the Mediterranean blended in. *Agro dolce* is Italian for sweet and sour, and the sour here comes in the form of sherry vinegar. I've also included a generous slurp of good olive oil, to give depth and extra flavour.

110 g (4 oz) stoned dried dates, chopped
2½ tablespoons sherry vinegar
3 tablespoons olive oil
½ teaspoon salt
1 mild red chilli, deseeded and chopped
250 ml (8 fl oz) water

Put all the ingredients into a saucepan and simmer for 10 minutes, then purée in a liquidizer. Serve cold.

Masala Mushy Peas

East meets the East End, Asia meets eel and pie shop, right common, right good and right cheap. Chunky old dried marrowfat peas, cooked in the way that you might make a dal, but you can't call it dal because that means 'split', as in split beans, and these little blighters are most definitely whole. The peas are simmered with turmeric, then finished with a *tarka* or *tadka* – in other words a mixture of hot oil, spices, onion and garlic all sizzled up together.

340 g (12 oz) marrowfat peas, soaked overnight
½ teaspoon ground turmeric
2–3 tablespoons fresh coriander leaves
salt

For the tarka

125 ml (4 fl oz) sunflower or vegetable oil
a pinch of asafoetida (optional)
1 teaspoon cumin seeds
4 garlic cloves, sliced
1 small onion, chopped
2 tomatoes, skinned, deseeded and chopped
1 red chilli, deseeded and finely chopped

Put the drained marrowfat peas into a saucepan with the turmeric and 1.2 litres (2 pints) water. Bring up to the boil, then reduce the heat and simmer, half-covered, for about 40 minutes, until the peas are tender enough to squash against the sides of the pan. Either crush about half the peas with a potato masher, in their juice, or use a small hand blender, to give a thick soupy mixture that retains some whole peas. Season generously with salt.

To make the tarka, heat the oil in a small frying pan over a moderate heat. Add the asafoetida, if using, give one stir, then add the cumin seeds. Give them a few seconds, then add the garlic and onion. Fry briskly for a few minutes, stirring frequently, until the onion has browned. Now add the tomatoes and chilli and stir until the tomato is soft. Tip the contents of the pan into the peas (reheated thoroughly, if necessary) and stir. Serve hot, sprinkled with the fresh coriander leaves.

Following page
(Clockwise from bottom centre): Onion and Almond Bhajis with Agro Dolce Date Sauce; Roast Roots and Alliums with Gentle Indian Spicing; Onion Cachumber; Naan Bread with Coriander Pesto; Mint, Grape and Cucumber Raita

Seared Spiced Salmon Fillet with Herb Butter

This is the most expensive recipe in the book and I make no apologies for the fact that the ingredients tot up to more than a fiver. This, after all, is meant to be a special occasion, and just once in a while it's worth splashing out. Besides, these days, salmon is cheaper than cod and, being an oily fish full of omega-3 fatty acids, it is also phenomenally good for you.

The salmon fillet is enhanced with a light spice rub, which gives flavour and somehow diminishes the rather earthy taste that farmed salmon can have. It is served with a straightforward herb butter enlivened with coriander, mint and methi. If you have never tried methi (fresh fenugreek leaves), then I urge you to give them a go. You can buy them in appealingly large bunches from Indian shops and stalls, and they have a surprising, curry-like scent. If you can't get methi, however, parsley can be used instead.

Any left-over methi could be used with potatoes (try adding a big handful to a pan of sautéed potatoes and frying for a minute or two longer) or scattered generously over a spatchcocked chicken, seasoned with lemon juice, olive oil, salt and pepper, then roasted in the oven, covered with foil for the first half of the cooking time.

When it comes to cooking the salmon, don't overdo it. Leave the fish a little underdone in the centre and you will be amazed by its juiciness and the improvement in taste.

6 portions of salmon fillet, weighing 110–175 g (4–6 oz) each
a little sunflower or vegetable oil

For the spice rub
1 teaspoon fennel seeds
a good pinch of fenugreek seeds
1 teaspoon cumin seeds
¼–½ teaspoon cayenne pepper
¼ teaspoon ground turmeric
2 garlic cloves, crushed
juice of ½–1 lime
salt and pepper

For the herb butter
2 tablespoons chopped fresh methi (fenugreek leaves)
2 tablespoons chopped fresh coriander
2 tablespoons chopped fresh mint
110 g (4 oz) softened unsalted butter
finely grated zest of ½ lime
1 tablespoon lime juice
salt and pepper

To make the spice rub, dry-fry the fennel, fenugreek and cumin seeds in a small frying pan over a moderate heat until they begin to crackle and turn a shade darker. Tip into a grinder and leave to cool. Add the cayenne and turmeric and grind all the spices together to a powder. Add the garlic, salt and pepper and enough lime juice to mix to a thick paste. Smear the spice rub over the salmon fillets, then cover and set aside for at least half an hour, preferably longer.

To make the herb butter, put all the ingredients into a food processor and process until evenly mixed. If you don't have a processor, chop the herbs very finely and beat them into the butter with all the remaining ingredients. Put the butter on a sheet of foil and form into a sausage shape, about 2.5–4 cm (1–1½ inches) thick. Roll up and chill in the fridge until needed.

Shortly before you intend to eat, put a heavy frying pan or griddle on to heat over a high flame. Brush the skin side of the salmon portions with a little oil. When the pan is horribly hot, lay the salmon pieces in it skin-side down. Leave, without nudging or moving them, for 3 minutes. Brush the upper side of the salmon with oil, then turn over and give the salmon another 3–4 minutes on the other side, so that it is almost cooked right through, but not quite. In other words, the centre should still be a little translucent with a bright rosy-pink colour – this will ensure juicy, moist fish.

Slice the chilled butter into discs, lay 2 or 3 discs on each piece of salmon, and serve immediately.

Roast Roots and Alliums with Tamarind

Roasting vegetables brings out all that is best in them, intensifying their natural flavours and caramelizing their sugar to a wonderful degree. All I've done here is add the fruity tartness of tamarind (available in blocks from Asian shops, which is much cheaper than buying the ready-made liquid now sold in some supermarkets) and spiced the roots and alliums (onions and garlic) with a touch of golden turmeric, cumin seeds and the nutty, coal-black seeds of black onion, also known as kalonji or nigella.

30 g (1 oz) tamarind
150 ml (¼ pint) very hot water
6 carrots, cut in half lengthways
12 small new potatoes (halve them if large)
3 large parsnips, cut into quarters lengthways and cored
3 red onions, quartered
1 head of garlic, divided into cloves but not peeled
4 tablespoons sunflower oil
½ teaspoon ground turmeric
2 teaspoons cumin seeds
1 teaspoon black onion seeds
coarse sea salt and lots of freshly ground black pepper

Pre-heat the oven to 220°C/425°F/Gas Mark 7.

Put the tamarind into a bowl and pour over the hot water. Leave to soak for about 20 minutes, mashing the tamarind pulp down with a fork every now and then. Give it one final squish and mash and mix, then rub the liquid through a sieve, pressing through as much of the soft tamarind pulp as will be parted from the seeds and fibres. Stir the tamarind liquid.

Put all the ingredients, including the tamarind liquid, into a roasting tin. Turn the vegetables to coat them in the oil and tamarind mixture. Cover with foil and cook in the oven for 20 minutes. Remove the foil, give the vegetable a good stir, then return to the oven and roast for a further 45–50 minutes, stirring once or twice, until they are all very tender and patched with brown. Serve hot or warm.

Stir-Fried Spinach with Cashew Nuts, Currants and South Indian Spices

This is definitely a last-minute dish, to be tossed together speedily, preserving the unique green taste of lightly cooked spinach. It is a marriage of Spanish/Italian dishes of spinach with pine kernels and currants, and Asian spices and nuts, bound together by a Chinese cooking method and a finishing flourish of Thai fish sauce. If you have the smallest liking for spinach, then please try it. It is outstandingly good.

Fresh curry leaves are available from some good Asian food stores and market stalls but if you can't get them, just leave them out. For this dish, dried curry leaves are not a good option.

450 g (1 lb) fresh spinach
3 tablespoons olive oil
a handful of curry leaves (optional)
1 teaspoon black mustard seeds
1 teaspoon cumin seeds
60 g (2 oz) cashew nuts
3 garlic cloves, chopped
1 fresh red chilli, deseeded and chopped
30 g (1 oz) currants
a good shake of Thai fish sauce (*nam pla*)
freshly ground black pepper

Rinse the spinach thoroughly, remove larger, tougher stalks, then dry the leaves well. You'll need to cook this quantity of spinach in 2 batches, so divide all the ingredients in half and arrange them around the stove. Put a wok over a high heat and leave until smoking. Spoon half the olive oil into the wok, pause for a second or two, then add half the curry leaves, if using, half the mustard seeds, cumin seeds, nuts, garlic and chilli, and stir-fry for about 30 seconds. Now add half the currants, followed by half the spinach. Stir-fry the spinach,

turning it enthusiastically, so that all the other ingredients mix in and the moisture in the leaves evaporates as soon as it seeps out, until the leaves are just wilting – this will take around 3–4 minutes, depending on the heat. Season with a few shakes of fish sauce and freshly ground black pepper. Stir to mix. Quickly tip out into a warm serving dish and keep warm while you cook the second half of the spinach. Serve immediately.

Mint, Grape and Cucumber Raita

Greek tzatziki meets Indian raita with a sunny hint of Mediterranean sweetness from the grapes. Serve this yoghurty side dish as a soothing, harmonizing addition to the main courses.

½ cucumber, peeled and finely diced
250 g (9 oz) Greek yoghurt
25 seedless white grapes, quartered
16 mint leaves
a pinch of paprika
salt and pepper

Put the cucumber into a colander and sprinkle lightly with salt. Leave to drain for half an hour, then rinse and pat dry on kitchen paper. Stir into the yoghurt with the grapes. Shred 14 of the mint leaves and stir those in too, then season with pepper. Taste and adjust the seasoning, adding salt only if you feel it really needs it. Just before serving, stir the raita again and spoon into a serving dish. Garnish with a light dusting of paprika and the reserved mint leaves.

Naan Bread with Coriander Pesto

I'd better warn you straight away that these do not turn out like the naan bread that you get in Indian restaurants – they taste even better, but the shape is quite different. That characteristic teardrop shape is produced by gravity and heat, as restaurant naans are cooked on the wall of a searingly hot tandoori oven. At home, the best results are achieved by cooking them horizontally, on a hot griddle – so no gravity, just a few seconds of puffing and mottled browning on either side.

To make them even more delicious, I've filled each one with a layer of coriander and coconut pesto, which incidentally is lovely tossed into noodles or stir-fried vegetables, or just used as a dip. Both the bread dough and the pesto can be made in advance but it is better to leave the rolling out and cooking to no more than 45 minutes before serving. Once they are cooked, keep the naans warm until ready to eat.

450 g (1 lb) strong white bread flour
1 teaspoon salt
1 sachet of easy-blend yeast
2 tablespoons sunflower oil
about 300 ml (½ pint) water

For the pesto

½ big bunch of fresh coriander
60 g (2 oz) hazelnuts, lightly toasted
3 garlic cloves, roughly chopped
45 g (1½ oz) creamed coconut, roughly chopped
90 ml (3 fl oz) sunflower or vegetable oil
salt and pepper

First make the dough. Put the flour into a bowl with the salt and yeast and mix evenly. Add the oil and rub it in with your fingers as though you were making pastry. Add enough water to mix to a soft, very slightly sticky dough. Turn the dough out and knead vigorously, dusting with a little extra flour if necessary, for a good 5–10 minutes, until silky smooth and elastic. Return to the bowl, cover with a damp cloth and leave in a warm place until doubled in size. This should take around an hour, or more depending on the warmth.

Meanwhile, make the coriander pesto. Cut off the coriander leaves – you should end up with about 50–60 g (1¾–2 oz). Put the coriander leaves, nuts, garlic and creamed coconut into a food processor with some salt and pepper. Process until smooth, then gradually trickle in the oil to form a smooth, thick sauce. Taste and adjust the seasoning, exaggerating it a touch.

When the dough has risen, punch it back, knead briefly, then divide into 6. Roll each piece into a ball on a floured surface, then roll out as thinly as you can to form a circle about 15 cm (6 inches) across. Smear a tablespoon of pesto over one half, leaving a 1 cm (½ inch) border around the edge. Brush the border with water, then fold the dough in half to cover the pesto entirely. Pinch the edges together firmly, then roll the naan out again to form a pointed oval, about 20 cm (8 inches) long. Don't worry too much if a bit of the pesto squidges out, but aim to keep most of it inside.

Place a heavy-based frying pan or griddle over a medium-high heat. Let it heat through for about 4 minutes, then lay the first naan on it and cook for 30–60 seconds, until it is beginning to puff and the underneath is spotted with brown dots. Turn over and cook the other side in the same way. Keep warm, loosely covered in the oven, while you cook the other naan breads.

Onion Cachumber

Another small side dish that makes a big difference. The sweet, juicy vigour of raw onion is enhanced by the paprika and lime juice to make the simplest of fresh chutneys.

1 large onion, chopped	
¼ teaspoon paprika	
a pinch of cayenne pepper	
juice of ½–1 lime	
a pinch of salt	

Mix all the ingredients together, using the juice of just half a lime. Taste and add more lime juice if needed.

Poached Starfruit

There was a bit of a craze for starfruit back in the Eighties, I think, but it didn't last that long. The reason is simple. Though they look enchantingly pretty when sliced, the perky yellow stars taste of very little. However, you can remedy that easily by poaching them in a sugar syrup. A touch of heat transforms their negligible culinary value, bringing an intriguing flavour to the fruit. And of course, they still look just as pretty. On Leicester market they sell three starfruit for a mere 50 pence, so I just couldn't resist. Once they'd been cooked and cooled in their syrup, I arranged some of them, along with a little of the syrup, around the coconut jelly (see page 102).

2 starfruit (carambola)	
175 g (6 oz) caster sugar	
425 ml (14 fl oz) water	

Slice the starfruit thinly, discarding the end pieces. Put the sugar into a pan with the water. Stir over a moderate heat until the sugar has dissolved, then bring up to the boil. Add the starfruit slices and reduce the heat. Poach gently for about 10 minutes, until the starfruit are tender. Take them out with a draining or slotted spoon and place in a shallow dish. Boil the syrup down hard until reduced by about half. Pour it over the starfruit and leave to cool. Serve with the jelly and kulfi.

Mango and Lime Kulfi

Kulfi is an ice-cream made with milk that has been cooked down to thicken and slightly caramelize the sweet milk solids. Mango kulfi, with the reduced milk mixed with puréed mangoes, is, unsurprisingly, one of the most popular types, and if you can lay your hands on fragrant, ripe, juicy, orange-fleshed mangoes it is easy enough to make.

If you want to prepare a seriously good, authentic kulfi, then you will take the time to boil fresh milk down from scratch. The trouble with this is that it has an infuriating tendency to catch on the base of the pan and burn. Far easier for the home cook, unused to such things, to shorten the whole process by starting off with evaporated milk, just reducing it enough to thicken slightly. Take it gently and be sure to use a heavy-based pan, which will conduct heat evenly.

The amount of sugar needed depends on the ripeness and variety of the mangoes.

5 ripe mangoes
juice of 2 limes
2 x 400 g (14 oz) tins of evaporated milk
85–110 g (3–4 oz) caster sugar

Peel the mangoes and cut all the flesh from the stones. Place in a food processor with the lime juice and blitz to a pulp. You should end up with about 900 g (2 lb) mango purée. Scrape into a bowl and chill until needed.

Put the evaporated milk into a heavy-based saucepan and bring up to the boil. Reduce the heat to low and cook gently for 15 minutes, stirring non-stop to prevent catching. Add the sugar and stir until dissolved, then draw off the heat. Leave to cool.

Turn the freezer to its coldest setting. When the milk is cool, gradually beat it into the mango purée, then either freeze in an ice-cream maker or pour into a shallow freezer container and pop into the freezer. Once the sides have set solid but the centre is still liquid, take it out of the freezer and break up the sides, pushing them into the centre. Repeat once, then leave to freeze until solid but not rock hard. Scrape the kulfi into the food processor and process to a smooth slush. If you don't have a food processor, beat it hard to smooth out jagged ice crystals. Pour the slush back into the container and return to the freezer. Transfer from the freezer to the fridge about half an hour before serving, to soften.

Note

If you have access to an Indian shop, you can buy special conical kulfi moulds. Pour the mixture into these when you have reached the processed slush stage, or from the ice-cream maker, and quickly freeze until solid.

Cardamom Coconut Jelly with Vark

This may be a banquet for grown-ups but I reckon that no good birthday party is complete without jelly and ice-cream. With that in mind, I came up with this scented combination of coconut milk jelly with cardamom seeds, served with mango kulfi (Indian ice-cream). Once you've made the coconut milk – home-made (see page 18), from either a fresh coconut or desiccated coconut, is infinitely preferable to tinned with its slimy texture – the jelly is child's play.

Vark is edible gold or silver leaf. It is pounded so very thin that it can be eaten almost without noticing, but it does add a beautiful and unusual finishing touch to the jelly. I buy pure silver leaf by mail-order (see page 158), but if you ask around in Indian sweet shops you may be able to find sources in towns with a strong Asian community.

Leaf gelatine is a little more costly than powdered gelatine but it is so much easier to use that I reckon it pays its way. It is sold by some larger supermarkets and good delicatessens. It is important to remember to stir the jelly occasionally as it cools, otherwise you will find an unsightly and unappealing crust of coconut cream forming on the top.

8 green cardamom pods
8 gelatine leaves
1.2 litres (2 pints) coconut milk (see page 18)
110 g (4 oz) caster sugar
1 sheet of vark (optional)

Slit open the cardamom pods, extract the seeds and crush them finely in a mortar and pestle or in a sturdy bowl with the end of a rolling pin. Half fill a roasting tin with cold water and lay the gelatine leaves in it, gently pushing them down under the surface. Put the coconut milk, crushed cardamom and sugar into a pan and stir over a moderate heat. Bring gently up to a boil, then draw off the heat. One by one, take the gelatine leaves out of the water, sloughing off the excess, and stir them into the hot coconut milk. Strain the milk through a fine sieve into a bowl and leave to cool. When it is cool, place in the fridge and leave until the mixture has the consistency of egg whites, stirring every 20 minutes or so. At this point, whisk it vigorously and pour into a 1.2 litre (2 pint) jelly mould, rinsed out with cold water. Return to the fridge and leave to set.

To unmould, dip the jelly mould briefly into a bowl of hot water – just a few seconds if the mould is made of metal, or some 20–30 seconds for a china mould. Run a fine-bladed knife around the upper edge of the mould and invert on to a plate. Grasp firmly and give the whole ensemble a firm shake. Once you've heard the satisfying plop of the jelly descending on to the plate, lift the mould off.

If you have managed to track down some vark, here is how to use it. First of all, take great care not to touch it with your fingers: it is so delicate that it will stick and tear. Arm yourself with a clean fine paintbrush. Without touching the vark, lift one sheet on its backing paper, and then quickly invert it on to the crown of the jelly. Lift off the backing paper to reveal the silver top. Using the paintbrush, lightly dab down any bits that are sticking up. Depending on the shape of the mould, you can also use some of the poached starfruit for added decoration.

Serve the jelly in its full shining glory.

Louise's Lime and Ginger Birthday Cake

Neil really went to town when he settled down to making Louise's birthday cake. He jazzed up a plain cake mixture by adding lime zest and fresh ginger, and sharpened an American cream cheese frosting with lime juice. Then he really pulled out all the stops. A quick raid on an Indian sweetmeat shop produced a box of bright orange *jalebis* (coiled, Indian syrup-soaked fritters) and some silver-topped *kaju katri* – lozenge-shaped sweetmeats made with cardamom and cashew nuts. With a flourish, these became part of the cake, bringing colour, drama and Eastern promise in their wake.

Though it was the Indian sweets that turned the cake into a vividly memorable masterpiece, for those of you who cannot buy them near where you live I can assure you that the cake itself was very good to eat anyway.

175 g (6 oz) butter, softened
175 g (6 oz) caster sugar
3 eggs, beaten
175 g (6 oz) self-raising flour, sifted
grated zest of 1 lime
2.5 cm (1 inch) fresh root ginger, peeled and finely grated

For the frosting
200 g (7 oz) cream cheese
110 g (4 oz) butter, softened
225 g (8 oz) icing sugar
juice of 1 lime

To decorate (optional)
250 g (9 oz) *jalebis*
5 *kaju katri* or other decorative, colourful Indian sweetmeats

Pre-heat the oven to 180°C/350°F/Gas Mark 4.

Cream the butter and sugar together until light and fluffy, then gradually beat in the eggs. Don't worry if the mixture looks a bit curdled – it will turn out all right in the end. Fold in the flour carefully, then the lime zest and ginger. Divide between 2 greased 20 cm (8 inch) sandwich tins. Level the tops and bake for 20–25 minutes, until a skewer inserted into the centre comes out clean. Turn out on to wire racks to cool.

To make the frosting, beat the cream cheese with the butter until well mixed, then gradually work in the icing sugar. Beat in the lime juice.

Use about a quarter of the frosting to sandwich the 2 cakes together. Dollop the rest on top of the cake and use a palette knife to smooth it over the top and down the sides. Don't even attempt to get it perfectly flat and even – this kind of frosting is meant to look ruffled. Press *jalebis* in all around the sides, if using, then decorate the top with the *kaju katri*.

3

Size does matter – menu for four

Polpettone con **Formaggio – Monster Meatballs** with **Melting Hearts**

Pear and **Cranberry Oat Crisp**

In our household, size matters enough to become a point of debate – on one issue at any rate, and that is the relative merits of giant and mini meatballs. Meatballs are by far and away my children's favourite dish, or at least they have met with their gobbling seal of approval with unswerving constancy over a period of years, which is quite something. The normal highly rated meatball is a small affair, something between a hazelnut and a walnut in size, so it was with trepidation that I presented these monster meatballs. I need not have worried – for we all decided that they compared favourably with the small ones. Now when I suggest meatballs for supper, discord breaks out, all size-related. The promise of what is, in effect, a crumble with oats seeded into the topping for pudding, smoothes down the ruffles, and by the time everyone is sitting round the table tucking in, heated discussion has turned to other, more weighty matters.

Since these two recipes tot up, by my reckoning, to a little under £4.50, you might well want to add a helping of greenery to the meatballs.

Polpettone con Formaggio – Monster Meatballs with Melting Hearts

These big, big meatballs have a small secret hidden away inside – a wee pool of molten cheese which oozes out as you cut into them. As long as you are careful during the initial frying (the two key tips are to make sure that the oil is good and hot and then not to fiddle around with them until they've browned underneath), they are very easy to cook. They make an excellent main course for a family supper or lunch, as people of all ages seem to love them. Serve them with some sort of greenery – lightly cooked Savoy cabbage, perhaps, or a green salad – and, if you can bear to go a little over the £5 barrier, add a generous bowlful of buttery mash, or noodles, or some baked potatoes.

60 g (2 oz) white bread without crusts, torn up	
500 g (1 lb 2 oz) minced pork	
2 garlic cloves, crushed	
1 tablespoon finely chopped parsley	
1 tablespoon finely chopped marjoram	
1 tablespoon finely chopped chives	
a little flour for dusting	
30 g (1 oz) strong Cheddar cheese, cut into 4 cubes	
2 tablespoons olive or sunflower oil	
400 g (14 oz) tin of tomatoes, chopped in their tin	
2 tablespoons tomato purée	
4 tablespoons water	
1 teaspoon caster sugar	
salt and pepper	

Soak the bread in cold water for about 3 minutes. Drain and squeeze out excess water firmly. Add the bread to the pork, along with the garlic, herbs, salt and pepper. Using your hands, mix and squelch it all together thoroughly to form a cohesive, mouldable mixture.

Divide the mixture into 4. Dust your hands with flour. Take the first portion of meatball mixture and roll it into a ball. Use your finger to hollow out a hole leading right to the centre of the ball. Insert a cube of Cheddar and then use your fingers and hands to close up the hole securely. Repeat with the remaining meatball mixture and cheese. If you have time, chill the meatballs for half an hour or so before cooking.

Heat the oil in a heavy-based frying pan over a fairly high heat. Add the meatballs, then let them sit, without moving, for 2–3 minutes, until they roll over easily if you shake the pan gently. Repeat until nicely browned all over. Pour in the tomatoes and all the remaining ingredients. Stir around the meatballs and bring up to the boil. Reduce the heat to a quiet simmer, then cover the pan with a lid, or a dome of

silver foil, and leave to cook gently for about 30 minutes, turning the meatballs carefully once in a while. If the sauce still seems a bit watery, remove the lid or foil and boil down for a few minutes longer. Taste and adjust the seasoning, then serve.

Pear and Cranberry Oat Crisp

A crisp, in this particular sweet-toothed sense of the word, is an American version of crumble. Since this pudding contains all-American cranberries mixed in with the pears, the name is particularly apt. If by any chance you leave out the cranberries, add another pear and reduce the sugar a little.

3 pears, peeled, cored and thickly sliced	
110 g (4 oz) cranberries	
1 teaspoon ground cinnamon	
3 cloves	
85 g (3 oz) caster sugar	

For the topping		
175 g (6 oz) plain flour		
60 g (2 oz) rolled oats		
a pinch of salt		
85 g (3 oz) butter, diced		
150 g (5 oz) caster sugar		

Pre-heat the oven to 190°C/375°F/Gas Mark 5.

Mix the pears, cranberries, cinnamon, cloves and caster sugar together and tip into a shallow ovenproof dish – I use a round dish 23 cm (9 inches) in diameter. For the topping, mix the flour with the oats and salt. Rub in the butter until the mixture resembles coarse breadcrumbs, then stir in the sugar. Scatter the crisp crumbs over the fruit in a thick, even blanket. Bake for 30–40 minutes, until browned and bubbling. Serve hot or warm.

menu

4

Poor man's revenge – menu for two

Poor Man's Asparagus

Turkey Schnitzel

Glazed Turnips and **Carrots**

Rice Pudding Brûlée

This menu takes its name from the first course, leeks vinaigrette, aka Poor Man's Asparagus. That's what my mother called them, and with good reason. It is one of the best of all ways to eat leeks, lifting them straight out of the realms of the ordinary-verging-on-dull, or worse (think of awful, gluey, soggy leeks in white sauce) into the aristocracy of the vegetable world, on a par with noble asparagus. The whole menu runs in the same vein: schnitzel are traditionally made with expensive veal but replace that with turkey and you have something quite delicious for a fraction of the price; and when it comes to crème brûlée, this poor man's version is a creamy rice pudding finished with the same crunch of caramelized sugar. You don't need buckets of money to eat well, and this menu, a poor man's pastiche of costlier foods, proves it.

Poor Man's Asparagus

This poor man is not to be pitied, for if he can dine on leeks vinaigrette he will have plenty to savour. This is one of those simple, classic dishes that definitely adds up to more than the sum of its parts. Make it several hours in advance to allow the leeks to drink in some of the vinaigrette, and serve at room temperature.

4 medium leeks
1 hard-boiled egg, shelled
1 tablespoon chopped parsley

For the dressing
3 tablespoons olive oil
1 tablespoon white wine vinegar
1 garlic clove, crushed
½ teaspoon Dijon mustard
salt and pepper

Trim the leeks and wash them thoroughly. Lay them in a wide pan with enough boiling salted water to come half way up the leeks. Bring back to the boil, then cover and simmer gently until tender, turning them once – allow about 8–10 minutes.

Meanwhile put all the dressing ingredients in a jam jar and shake well to mix.

Drain the leeks really thoroughly; watery leeks will spoil practically any dish and this one is no exception. While they are still warm, arrange them in a serving dish and pour over the dressing. Turn them carefully until they are nicely coated. Set aside to cool down. While they cool, mash up the hard-boiled egg with a fork into tiny crumbs. Shortly before serving, scatter the leeks with the egg and parsley.

Turkey Schnitzel

Veal is still a meat that people in this country are wary of using, which is a shame because it can taste superb, and these days it is relatively easy to find home-produced, humanely reared veal. When you do come across it (and you can tell humanely raised veal by its rosy pink colour) it tends to be rather expensive – restaurants snap up all the best cuts. For a dish like this, turkey makes an acceptable alternative – not the same, to be sure, but with the help of a little ham and the crisp crumbed exterior, that's hardly likely to be a problem.

60 g (2 oz) fresh breadcrumbs
1 tablespoon finely chopped parsley
1 egg
30 g (1 oz) plain flour
¼ teaspoon each salt and pepper
2 turkey breast steaks, weighing around 110 g (4 oz) each
1 thick slice of ham (weighing around 45 g/1½ oz), cut in half
30 g (1 oz) butter
1 tablespoon sunflower oil
½ lemon

Mix the breadcrumbs and parsley together. Beat the egg with ½ tablespoon of water. Season the flour with the salt and pepper and spread it out on a plate. Cut a pocket in each turkey breast and put half the ham in each pocket. Sandwich the breasts between 2 sheets of greaseproof paper and beat with a rolling pin until slightly flattened (a great way to work out the stresses of the day, but don't go overboard if it's been a bad one). Dip the two turkey 'schnitzels' first in the flour, shaking off the excess, then in the egg and finally turn them in the breadcrumb mixture, making sure that they are thoroughly covered on both sides. Chill for half an hour.

When you are nearly ready to eat, melt the butter with the oil in a large heavy frying pan over a moderate heat. Fry the crumbed turkey for 4–5 minutes on each side, until appetizingly golden brown. Cut the lemon half in half again and serve a wedge of lemon with each schnitzel.

Glazed Turnips and Carrots

If you have ever been a touch iffy about turnips (and you are amongst good company), give them another go. If you are partial to turnips, as I am, then you won't need any encouragement to try this recipe. The initial cooking takes away any residual bitterness, while the final reheating in butter and a touch of sugar brings out their true heart of gold. The buttery sweetness emphasizes the inherent sweet, earthy flavour of the carrots. Of course, the other great advantage of cooking them this way is that the vegetables can be prepared and simmered in advance, then finished off at the last minute, just before you tuck in.

225 g (8 oz) carrots
225 g (8 oz) turnips
30 g (1 oz) butter
1 tablespoon caster sugar
salt

Cut the carrots and turnips into batons about 5 mm (¼ inch) thick and 4 cm (1½ inches) long. Simmer gently in salted water until just tender, then drain thoroughly.

Melt the butter in the saucepan and return the carrots and turnips to it. Sprinkle over the sugar. Sauté gently until the vegetables are lightly browned and glossy from the butter and sugar. Taste and adjust the seasoning, then serve immediately.

Rice Pudding Brûlée

I have a bit of a thing about rice pudding and I'm not afraid to admit it. I love the stuff and always have. I even liked school rice pudding (and the prunes that came with it, but that's another story ...). Never fear, this is nothing like it. Under the crisp shell of caramelized sugar awaits an idyll of soft, tender grains in creamy cooked-down milk, with an elusive, almondy flavour that may puzzle the unknowing. It comes from a bay leaf, which was used to flavour milk puddings in this country for centuries, until we consigned it to the realms of the savoury. Try it, and discover how unexpectedly good it can be.

Incidentally, these need to be made well in advance (in the morning for the evening, say) so that they have time to cool down twice over.

300 ml (½ pint) milk
1 bay leaf, snapped in half
30 g (1 oz) pudding rice
1 tablespoon caster sugar
15 g (½ oz) unsalted butter
2 tablespoons demerara sugar

Pour the milk into a pan and add the bay leaf. Bring slowly to the boil. Turn off the heat, cover and leave to infuse for half an hour. Remove the bay leaf and strain the milk on to the pudding rice in a second saucepan. Stir in the caster sugar, then bring up to the boil. Simmer gently for 20–30 minutes, stirring occasionally, until creamy. Grease two 150 ml (¼ pint) ramekins with the butter and pour in the rice mixture. Leave to cool.

Pre-heat the grill thoroughly. Sprinkle 1 tablespoon of demerara sugar over each ramekin and grill until the sugar melts and bubbles, which should take some 3–5 minutes. Leave to cool. As it cools, the sugar hardens to a solid crust. Serve the rice pudding brûlées either at room temperature or lightly chilled.

5

Know your *onions* – menu for four

Tatin of Caramelized Onions and **Garlic** with **Goat's Cheese Pastry**

Red Cabbage, Orange and **Black Olive Salad**

Fried Apricots with **Almonds** and **Whipped Cardamom Cream**

Goat's cheese is not cheap, there's no denying that, but when it is brought into play with oodles of slowly cooked caramelized onions and garlic, the pence all even themselves out to a very moderate expense. And it's that interplay of cheap and more costly that marks out this slightly unusual menu for four people. Red cabbage costs next to nothing, which makes up for the black olives that are one of life's small luxuries. Dried apricots are surprisingly expensive, though the price varies enormously from one supermarket to another (healthfood stores often sell them at very reasonable rates), but although cardamom pods and cream are considered extravagant, in small quantities they won't break the bank.

The other feature that marks this menu is a somewhat unorthodox approach to well-known ingredients – caramelizing onions and making them the focus of the dish instead of letting them fade into the background; stir-frying red cabbage for a salad instead of stewing it long and slow; and for heaven's sake, whoever came up with the crazy idea of frying dried apricots? Not me, I'm sorry to say ...

Following page
(From left to right):
Red Cabbage, Orange and Black Olive Salad; Tatin of Caramelized Onions and Garlic with Goat's Cheese Pastry; Fried Apricots with Almonds and Whipped Cardamom Cream

Tatin of Caramelized Onions and Garlic with Goat's Cheese Pastry

I doubt that the revered Tatin sisters appreciated what they were unleashing on the world when they created their famous caramelized upside-down apple tart. I imagine they soon realized that it was one of the best of all apple tarts, but could they have guessed that their surname would be appended to all manner of creations inspired by their original? Well, probably not, but here is yet another tribute to the sisters' magnificent invention – my take on the savoury tart Tatin and, though I say it myself, really rather a stunner.

The natural sweetness of onions and garlic is emphasized by caramelizing them gently, but the pastry counters it with the salty weight of goat's cheese. It's easy to make, with a touch of drama built in at the end as the pan is inverted to reveal the finished onion and garlic Tatin in all its full, glossy glory.

10 garlic cloves, peeled	
60 g (2 oz) unsalted butter	
3 onions, sliced	
60 g (2 oz) caster sugar	
1½ tablespoons red wine vinegar	
salt and pepper	

For the pastry

175 g (6 oz) plain flour	
¼ teaspoon salt	
85 g (3 oz) softened butter	
85 g (3 oz) rinded goat's cheese, crumbled	
1 teaspoon fresh thyme leaves	

To make the pastry, sift the flour with the salt. Beat the butter and goat's cheese together vigorously until well mixed and softened, then work in the thyme leaves and the sifted flour. Gather up into a ball, knead briefly to smooth out, then wrap in clingfilm and chill for at least half an hour.

Find a heavy-based ovenproof frying pan or cake tin about 25 cm (10 inches) in diameter. Roll the pastry out into a rough circle a tad larger than the frying pan or cake tin. Slide the pastry on to a baking sheet or large plate, cover loosely and return to the fridge until needed.

Pre-heat the oven to 190°C/375°F/Gas Mark 5.

Blanch the garlic cloves for 2 minutes in boiling salted water, then drain thoroughly. Melt the butter in the frying pan or tin, add the onions and garlic cloves and fry gently for about 5–7 minutes, until the onions are tender and the garlic cloves beginning to soften. Now sprinkle over the sugar, vinegar, a touch of salt and plenty of freshly ground black pepper. Stir and continue cooking for another 10 minutes or so, until both onions and garlic are very lightly caramelized. Draw off the heat and distribute the onions and garlic more or less evenly around the pan. Quickly lay the pastry on top of the onions and garlic, gently pressing it over them and tucking the edges down into the pan. Place in the oven and bake for about 20–30 minutes, until golden brown.

Take the tart out of the oven, then run a knife around the edge of the pan. Place a large plate on top and invert the whole caboodle in one swift motion. If any of the topping sticks to the pan, don't worry; scrape it off and spread it on the tart Tatin, and no one will be any the wiser. Serve at once while hot, or when just warm.

Red Cabbage, Orange and Black Olive Salad

I love that Germanic way of slowly cooking red cabbage with apple, spices, vinegar and sugar for several hours until it has reduced down to a glorious, purple, sweet-sour mass but, wonderful though that is, it's not the only way to deal with red cabbage. Swiftly stir-fried, it develops a fresh-tasting half-soft half-crisp texture that is enormously satisfying. You can season it Chinese-style, with plenty of garlic, spring onions, ginger and maybe a few shakes of soy sauce, and serve it hot, but it is also an excellent way of taking the rather insistently cabbagey, chewy edge off the raw vegetable for a lively salad. That's what I've done here and, to give colour and zip, I've added fresh pieces of orange and salty black olives. By the way, it really is a false economy to buy cheap stoned olives. They tend to taste soapy and rather unpleasant, and they don't keep as long as olives with their stones in.

¼ red cabbage
3 tablespoons olive oil
1 onion, thinly sliced
juice of ½ lemon
1 teaspoon Worcestershire sauce
a pinch of sugar
1 orange, peeled and thinly sliced
12 black olives
salt and pepper

Cut the thick core out of the cabbage and slice the rest very thinly. Heat the oil in a wok over a very high heat indeed. Add the cabbage and onion and stir-fry briskly, without reducing the heat, until it is soft and floppy but still has a slight crunch – about 5–6 minutes. Turn off the heat, add the lemon juice, Worcestershire sauce, sugar, salt and pepper and toss together. Let the mixture cool until tepid, then mix in the orange and black olives. Taste and adjust the seasoning. Serve at room temperature.

Fried Apricots with Almonds and Whipped Cardamom Cream

I can take little credit for this recipe. The seemingly mad idea of frying dried apricots is actually quite inspired, giving them a rich, slightly toasty flavour. I came across it when I was working on a television programme with the very talented chef Phil Vickery, and although I've made a few small, economy-driven changes to the recipe, the principle and method are lifted straight from him. Thanks, Phil.

24 ready-to-eat dried apricots
150 ml (¼ pint) whipping cream
15 g (½ oz) unsalted butter
15 g (½ oz) flaked almonds

For the syrup

4 cardamom pods
200 ml (7 fl oz) water
85 g (3 oz) caster sugar
4 strips of lemon zest
juice of 1 large lemon

Soak the apricots in water for at least 4 hours, longer if possible. Meanwhile, make the syrup. Slit open the cardamom pods, extract the seeds and crush them in a pestle and mortar or in a small bowl with the end of a rolling pin. Place them in a saucepan with all the remaining syrup ingredients. Bring up to the boil, stirring until the sugar has completely dissolved, and simmer for 3 minutes, then draw off the heat. Leave to cool, then strain. Whip the cream with 2 tablespoons of the syrup until it holds its shape softly. Chill until needed. Drain the apricots and pat dry. Heat the butter in a frying pan until foaming. Add the apricots and almonds and sauté on both sides until patched with brown. Now add the remainder of the syrup and bring up to the boil. Let it bubble hard until reduced by about half, turning the apricots in it. Serve the hot apricots immediately, topped with clouds of the chilled cream melting down over them.

6

Menu for a cold *winter's* day – for four

Daube of Beef with **Cannellini Beans** and **Rosemary**

Caramelized Oranges

Previous page
(From left to right):
Daube of Beef with
Cannellini Beans and
Rosemary; Caramelized
Oranges

It's a freezing cold winter's day but the sun is shining and the hoar frost on the trees sparkles like some enchanted forest. Don't waste it – go out for a long, invigorating walk, thrill to the beauty of it all, and then come back to this steaming-hot, densely savoury, comforting casserole of beef and beans, guaranteed to take the chill off your fingers. To finish, a classic light pudding that will refresh the palate, a bowl of caramelized oranges, glowing like jewels.

Daube of Beef with Cannellini Beans and Rosemary

One of the best cuts of beef for stewing just happens to be one of the cheapest. Shin of beef is veined with translucent folds between the muscle, which break down during long cooking to give a lip-smacking, gelatinous, velvety richness to the sauce. To that is added the mealy, softness of cannellini beans, slowly cooked to tenderness in the meaty juices. I've called this stew a daube because it is flavoured with the scents of the daubes, or casseroles, of southern France – most notably, rosemary and dried orange zest. You'll be amazed at the power of one lone strip of dried orange zest, so much stronger than a fresh strip. Make the pudding the day before if you can, and remember to take a strip of zest off one of the oranges so that it can dry overnight to be added to the daube.

225 g (8 oz) dried cannellini beans, soaked overnight in cold water
1 onion, chopped
2 carrots, diced
2 celery stalks, diced
2 tablespoons olive oil
4 garlic cloves, chopped
800–900 g (1¾–2 lb) shin of beef, cut into 4 cm (1½ inch) cubes
a bouquet garni made of 1 bay leaf, 3 sprigs of rosemary and 1 strip of dried orange peel, tied together with string
600 ml (1 pint) water
1 tablespoon tomato purée
2 tinned plum tomatoes, roughly chopped
salt and pepper

Pre-heat the oven to 150°C/300°F/Gas Mark 2. Drain the beans and rinse. Sauté the onion, carrots and celery in the oil until patched with brown. Add the garlic and cook for a minute or two longer. Place in an ovenproof casserole with the beans. Now brown the chunks of beef thoroughly in the remaining oil in the pan. Put them into the casserole as well, pushing them down among the beans and vegetables. Add the bouquet garni and season with pepper, but don't add any salt at this stage.

Pour excess fat off from the frying pan, then pour in the water. Bring up to the boil, scraping in the residues from frying the meat and the vegetables. When it is boiling, pour into the casserole and add enough hot water to just about cover the meat. Transfer to the oven and leave to cook for about 2 hours. Stir, and taste one of the beans to see if it is completely tender. If it is still a bit firm, return the stew to the oven for another half an hour or so, then try again. Once the beans are tender, stir in the tomato purée, chopped tomatoes and some salt. Return to the oven for a further 1–2 hours until the meat is incredibly tender and the sauce has reduced to a pleasing consistency. Taste and adjust the seasoning, then serve.

Caramelized Oranges

One of the great winter puddings, this. Sliced oranges, bathed in caramel. Nothing more and nothing less, yet tremendously good. I first came across it as a child, in an Italian restaurant my parents took me to every now and then. The sliced oranges, reformed into glistening orbs with the aid of cocktail sticks, reposed voluptuously on the dessert trolley. I've loved them ever since. After the comforting, filling nature of the daube, they cleanse and refresh the palate in the most seductive fashion.

On a more practical note, this pudding can be made a day or two in advance and keeps well in the fridge, covered with clingfilm.

4 oranges	
200 g (7 oz) caster sugar	
3 cloves	

Pare the zest from 2 oranges (you don't need the rest for this recipe, so if you are feeling thrifty, pare the zest from the last 2 oranges, thread it up in long skeins and leave to dry out so you can use it to flavour daubes, like the one above, and other meaty stews, as well as some Chinese-style dishes). Cut the zest into fine shreds, then blanch for 2 minutes in boiling water. Drain and reserve.

Peel all 4 oranges, cutting right down to the flesh with a sharp knife. Slice each orange, saving the juices that are squeezed out and discarding any pips that you happen across, then reassemble it in its original form and push a cocktail stick through the centre to hold the slices together. Place all the oranges in a shallow dish, together with the juice.

Put the sugar into a pan (use one with a metallic or white interior, not black, so that you can see the colour of the sugar clearly as it caramelizes) with 100 ml (3½ fl oz) water and cloves. Stir over a moderate heat until the sugar has completely dissolved. Bring up to the boil and stop stirring. Boil hard, swirling the pan occasionally to even out hot spots, but never stirring, until the sugar darkens to a hazelnut-brown caramel. Now, at arm's length, pour in 150 ml (¼ pint) hot water; it will spit. Swirl the pan, then stir to make a clear caramel sauce. Add the shreds of orange zest and simmer for about 10 minutes in the syrup until translucent. Pour the syrup and the shreds over the oranges, then leave to cool. Serve at room temperature or lightly chilled.

menu

7

A devilishly good *supper* for four

Devilled Drumsticks

Roast Carrot Salad

Banana Bread Pudding

Banana Teabread

This is a homely affair, this devilishly good supper, but not to be sneered at, for all that. The combination of sticky devilled drumsticks (actually not at all hot, unless you throw in a shake of Tabasco) with tender, slowly roasted carrots enlivened with mint and lemon juice, followed by an indulgent banana-laden version of bread and butter pudding is one that will bring a smile to most lips, once they've finished licking them.

Everything is cooked in the oven, which means that it is all relatively undemanding. Have a quick peak once or twice and give the drumsticks a baste, then read the newspaper or play ludo or whatever takes your fancy while you wait for it all to cook. If you can permit yourself a little extra expenditure, pop four baking potatoes into the oven with the drumsticks and carrots (a metal skewer pushed through the middle of each potato speeds up the cooking) to serve moistened with the juices left in the drumstick dish.

Devilled Drumsticks

The word devilled brings enticing notions of wickedness to any dish, so I hope you won't be too disappointed when you realize that this is just a recipe for drumsticks baked in the oven in a sweet, sticky marinade. These days, this might more commonly be thought of as a barbecue sauce, but the old-fashioned English term 'devilled', referring to the spice of the Worcestershire sauce and the mustard, is much more vivid. In winter, serve the devilled drumsticks hot from the oven, but when summer comes they make good picnic fare, eaten cold, or can be cooked on the barbecue, as long as they are frequently brushed with the marinade as they sizzle in the heat.

8 chicken drumsticks

For the marinade

1 tablespoon Worcestershire sauce

2 tablespoons tomato ketchup

2 tablespoons dark muscovado sugar

1 tablespoon dark soy sauce

3 garlic cloves, crushed

1 tablespoon Dijon or English mustard

½ tablespoon red or white wine vinegar

1 tablespoon sunflower oil

Mix together all the marinade ingredients. Arrange the drumsticks in a single layer in a shallow ovenproof dish and pour over the marinade. Turn the drumsticks to coat, then cover and leave to marinate for at least half an hour, longer if you can – up to 24 hours in the fridge. If the chicken has been in the fridge, though, let it come back to room temperature before cooking.

Pre-heat the oven to 200°C/400°F/Gas Mark 6.

Spoon the marinade over the drumsticks one more time, so that they are moist and evenly sozzled in it. Place the dish, drumsticks, marinade and all (but uncovered) in the oven, and bake for about 50 minutes, turning and basting the thighs roughly every 15 minutes so that they are browned and sticky all over. They can now be eaten hot from the oven, or left to cool in their juices and reheated thoroughly later, or eaten at room temperature.

Roast Carrot Salad

This is an old favourite of ours, but if you have never tasted roast carrots before it will come as something of a revelation. The dry heat of the oven intensifies their flavour, making them irresistibly delicious. Tossed with lemon juice, garlic and mint, then left to cool, they are sensationally good. Start them off in the oven about half an hour before the drumsticks, so that they cool to something near room temperature by the time you are ready to eat.

900 g (2 lb) large carrots, peeled

4 tablespoons olive oil

½ teaspoon coarse salt

2 small garlic cloves, finely chopped

juice of ½ large lemon

a handful of mint leaves, roughly torn up

freshly ground pepper

Pre-heat the oven to 200°C/400°F/Gas Mark 6.

Cut the carrots into 7.5 cm (3 inch) lengths. Halve the lower ends lengthways and cut the fatter upper ends into quarters lengthways. Put them all into a roasting tin or ovenproof dish with the oil and salt. Turn to coat the carrots evenly. Roast for about 45 minutes, turning occasionally, until very tender and patched with brown.

Tip the contents of the pan into a shallow serving dish and add all the remaining ingredients. Taste and add a little more salt if needed. Serve at room temperature.

Banana Bread Pudding

This is, in effect, bread and butter pudding for banana lovers. It is made from the Banana Teabread (see opposite), rather than a conventional loaf. You do have to make the teabread a day or two in advance but from then on it's plain sailing. In fact, you can even make the whole pudding the day before you want to eat it, because it is even nicer chilled than hot.

2 bananas
6 thin slices of Banana Teabread (see opposite)
15 g (½ oz) unsalted butter
2 eggs
30 g (1 oz) caster sugar
150 ml (¼ pint) double cream
150 ml (¼ pint) milk

Slice the bananas on the diagonal to form elongated oval slices. Spread the teabread lightly with the butter and make 3 banana sandwiches using the teabread and the bananas. Cut each sandwich in half diagonally to make triangles, and nestle, overlapping slightly like roof tiles, in a lightly buttered baking dish into which they fit fairly snugly. Scatter any left-over slices of banana among the sandwiches.

Whisk the eggs with the sugar until pale and thick. Put the cream and milk into a saucepan and bring up to the boil, then pour on to the eggs, whisking constantly. Pour the mixture over the banana sandwiches and leave for half an hour. Pre-heat the oven to 170°C/325°F/Gas Mark 3.

Bake the pudding for about 30–35 minutes, until barely set. Serve hot, warm or at room temperature, or even chilled the next day.

Banana Teabread

How many times have you thrown out the last few bananas because they've gone all brown and a bit squishy? And you must have seen past-their-prime bananas being sold off cheaply at the end of the day in markets and greengrocer's. Well, this is one excellent way to use up those sorry specimens of banana-hood, transforming them into a teatime banana bread that is gorgeous just sliced and buttered and superb toasted for breakfast. It is also an essential element of the pudding that brings this menu to its grand finale. One note of warning, however – if you are going to make the banana bread pudding you will need to bake the teabread the day before, so that it slices without crumbling and collapsing.

Makes 1 loaf – serves 8–10

300 g (10 oz) self-raising flour
1 level teaspoon baking powder
½ teaspoon ground cinnamon
¼ teaspoon salt
110 g (4 oz) light muscovado sugar
300 g (10 oz) peeled bananas (roughly 3 large ones)
2 teaspoons lemon juice
2 large eggs
1 teaspoon vanilla essence
175 ml (6 fl oz) sunflower oil
2 tablespoons poppy seeds

Pre-heat the oven to 180°C/350°F/Gas Mark 4.

Sift the flour with the baking powder, cinnamon and salt, then stir in the sugar. Mash the bananas with the lemon juice and beat in the eggs, vanilla essence and oil. Add to the dry ingredients and mix well, then stir in the poppy seeds. Pour into a greased

450 g (1 lb) loaf tin and bake for 55–65 minutes, until well risen and browned. Poke a skewer into the centre – if it comes out clean the teabread is done.

Turn out and leave to cool on a wire rack, then wrap in clingfilm or silver foil. Leave for at least 24 hours before eating. Serve sliced and buttered, but save some for the banana bread pudding.

8

Two Classic Winter *Preserves*

Boozy Marmalade

Seville Orange Curd

Who says there is no such thing as seasons any more? January sees the beginning of the brief reign of Seville oranges, but by mid or late February they are gone again. Enjoy them while they are around – use the tart, bitter, spicy juice to flavour sauces for fish, or in a baked custard to give it a unique citrus scent. Add it to marinades or squeeze a little into salad dressings. Above all, however, take the time to make marmalade. Home-made marmalade is vastly superior to most bought marmalades. Besides which, bought marmalades of a comparable quality are far more expensive. At this point I have to admit that I am not a keen marmalade eater, but that doesn't stop me knocking up a batch for friends who come to stay, or to give away as presents, and to feed the insatiable demands of school and village fêtes. The wafts of orange scent that float through the house as it boils away are a welcome bonus.

This year, however, I have discovered a new passion – Seville orange curd. It doesn't keep as long, but the particular aroma of Sevilles is balanced by the buttery richness of the curd itself. Fantastic.

Following page
(From left to right):
Seville Orange Curd;
Boozy Marmalade

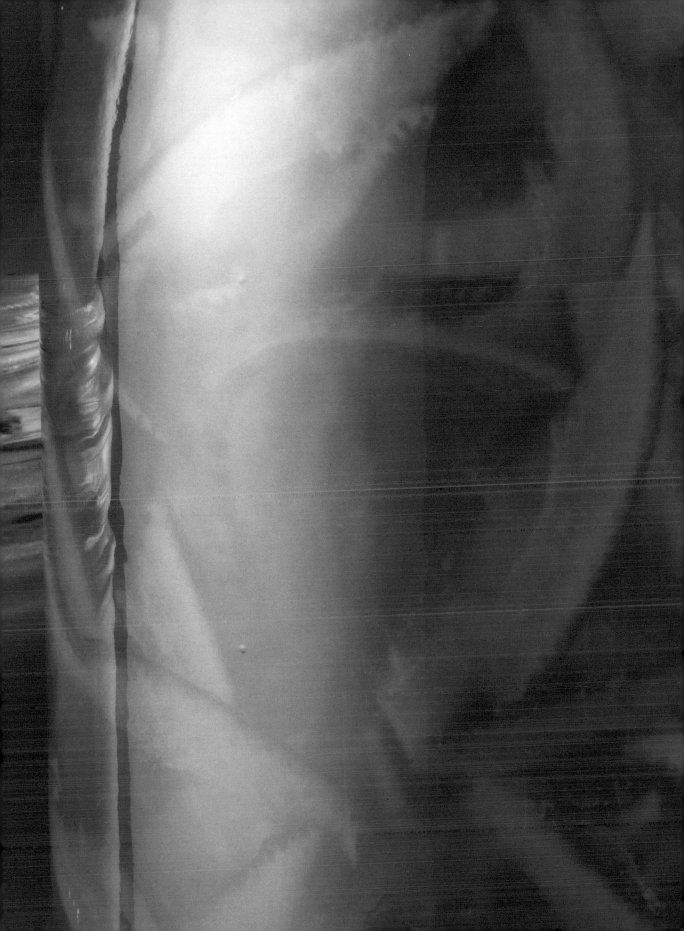

Boozy Marmalade

You don't have to add the alcohol to this marmalade but it sure starts the day off with a kick if you do. Actually, it works out as precious little booze per slice of toast, so no one need worry about weaving their way too merrily to work, but the flavour of the chosen spirit or liqueur spreads itself joyfully through the pots. Depending on the alcohol you use, the final bill works out at about 55–60 pence per jar.

Makes about 2.75–3 kg (6–7 lb)

1 kg (2¼ lb) Seville oranges
1 large lemon
2.25 litres (4 pints) water
1.8 kg (4 lb) granulated sugar
125 ml (4 fl oz) whisky, brandy, rum, cointreau or whatever other decent hooch you may have in the cupboard

Halve all the citrus fruit and squeeze out the juice, saving any pips and crushed flesh. Strain the juice into a preserving pan or a large, heavy-based saucepan. Take the lemon halves and cut them up roughly. Put the pieces, along with the reserved pips and flesh, on a square of muslin (or a J-cloth, rinsed out thoroughly in boiling water) and knot together tightly.

Now halve the orange halves and slice them very thinly into long shreds. Add them to the juice in the pan. Add the bag of pips and lemon peel, too. Pour in the water, and then bring up to the boil. Simmer for about 2 hours, stirring from time to time, until the orange peel is very soft and the liquid level has gone down by about one third. Take the bag of pips out of the pan, squeeze it hard against the side with a wooden spoon to extract the last of the goodness, then discard.

Meanwhile, warm the sugar gently in a low oven (this helps it dissolve more quickly). Add the warmed sugar to the pan of juice and peel and stir until completely dissolved. Boil hard until setting point is reached (see below). Draw off the heat and skim off any scum, then stir in the booze. Let the marmalade settle for about 3 minutes, then ladle into hot, sterilized jars (see below), seal tightly and label. Store in a cool, dark place.

To test for setting point

Before you begin making marmalade, jam or jelly, stash three or four saucers in the fridge. Start testing for a set fairly soon after the mixture, with the sugar in, has started to boil hard. Just drip a few drops on to one of the chilled saucers. Cool for a minute or two, then nudge one of the drops with your finger. If it wrinkles on the surface, your preserve has reached setting point and is ready to pot up. If the drop remains very runny, continue boiling for 5 minutes, then try again.

To sterilize jam jars

Wash the jars thoroughly in soapy water, then rinse well. Without touching the insides, turn them upside down and leave to dry on a rack in the oven set to 110°C/225°F/Gas Mark ¼ for at least half an hour, or longer. Unless otherwise indicated in the recipe, fill the jars straight from the oven, while they are still hot.

Seville Orange Curd

If you've never tasted home-made lemon curd, then you have missed out on one of the most delicious preserves in the world. This Seville orange curd is very special too, with the bitter tartness of the juice softened and tamed by the butter, sugar and eggs. Anyone who likes marmalade is bound to love it, and those who are not so keen on marmalade, like myself, take to it with alacrity, too.

If you want to make straight lemon curd, just substitute lemon juice and zest for the Seville juice and zest. Lime curd is fantastic too, but since limes are smaller than lemons but just as costly, it works out rather more expensive.

Seville, lemon and lime curds do not have the longevity of jams and jellies. Once cooled, store in the fridge for up to four weeks. If you plan to give it to anyone as a present, mark a use-by date on the label.

Makes around 1.3 kg (2½ lb)

9–12 Seville oranges
550 g (1¼ lb) caster sugar
225 g (8 oz) unsalted butter, diced
5 large eggs

One at a time, grate the zest of the Sevilles finely, then squeeze the juice and strain it into a measuring jug until you have 300 ml (½ pint). Pour into a bowl and add the zest, sugar and butter. Place the bowl over a pan of gently simmering water, making sure that the base of the bowl does not come into contact with the water. Stir until the butter is melted and the sugar has dissolved.

Beat the eggs lightly to loosen them, then strain through a sieve into the warm Seville orange and butter mixture. Stir constantly, over the gently simmering water, until the mixture has thickened enough to coat the back of a spoon – allow a good 20–25 minutes but take great care not to let the curds get anywhere near boiling point. Woe betide you if you let your attention wander for more than a few seconds, for overheated curds will curdle and scramble to an unsightly and ruined mess. Actually, this rarely happens in my experience (never, so far, though I guess there is always a first time ...) but remember my dire warnings nonetheless.

As soon as the mixture has thickened, lift the bowl out of the pan and pour the curd into warm, sterilized jars (see page 124). Seal tightly, label and leave to cool. Keep the curd in the fridge.

SPRING

A Wet Weekend in *Glasgow*

Spring has sprung to such an extent that the daffodils are fading, even here, right up north in Glasgow. I arrive on the most beautiful morning, blue skies beaming down the most enticing welcome. By lunchtime it has clouded over and that's the last of the sunshine until, annoyingly, I climb back onto the plane to leave. It's a good job I'm not superstitious, for one could take the pocket of scowling, wind-swept icy weather that settles in with me as some sort of bad omen. Luckily the chill of the outdoors is more than made up for by the warmth of the family I am about to meet. By the time I've made it to our rendezvous in the famous Willow Tea Rooms, the temperature outside has plummeted and I am delighted to escape into the remarkable Charles Rennie Mackintosh interior.

And here they all are, in the De Luxe room, ornately decorated with purple, pink and silver. Over tea we work our way through the business of getting to know the basics about ourselves. So, let me introduce you to the West family. Fiona and Stephen are both musicians, she plays the viola, he the cor anglais, with the Royal Scottish National Orchestra, based here in Glasgow. They have one young son, the mischievous Moray, who soon gets over his shyness to reveal himself as a typically high-spirited, cheeky four-year-old. Fiona's three daughters from a previous marriage, Rosina, Amy and Ailsa are also tucking into scones with enthusiasm, though Rosina has to return that afternoon to Loch Lomond where she works.

After tea the rest of us troop back to their house just outside the city, where I am introduced to the latest additions to the West clan: two vociferous budgies, and a rumbustious, affectionate black Labrador called Kyle. This is a household that seems to be permanently on the go. Fiona and Stephen's rehearsals usually take place at civilized times, but when they are performing in the theatre, they have to leave at 6 sharp. Moray goes to nursery school in the morning in the next-door village, and to a childminder in the afternoon. Amy, 17 and Ailsa, 14 amble in from school at around 4, and then, if they are not on baby-sitting duty, meander out again to see their friends a few hours later. Still, with all this activity, the atmosphere is one of enormous warmth and fun. Fiona bursts into fits of laughter at the drop of a hat and to the delight of the children, Stephen is a consummate prankster, armed with remote-control wind machine, and other equally silly tricks.

Fiona is a vegetarian, Stephen is not. All the children have initially been brought up as vegetarians but Amy is now Stephen's ally in the quest for meat, while Ailsa, who once embraced the sausage and chip culture, has returned to her vegetarian roots. Moray has not yet encountered meat. Into this lively, upbeat household, I am pitched as guest cook for two days. Quite a challenge – but one that I can see is going to be enormous fun.

1

After *school* meal for four

Nettle Soup

Fiona's Spinach and **Feta Pie**

Carrot and **Raisin Salad**

It's not easy juggling meals, work, and childcare when both parents are musicians in a high-powered orchestra like the RSNO. Luckily for Fiona and Stephen, the girls are now old enough to look after their little brother, Moray, when they can't be there in the evenings. But Fiona still has to make sure that they have good, enticing and nutritious food to tuck into. A Greek-style spinach and feta pie is an old favourite, much enjoyed by both vegetarian and carnivorous siblings, but nettle soup is a relatively new discovery. In fact, the recipe is based on one of my mother's, from *Jane Grigson's Vegetable Book*. The family pick the nettles in a wood just up the lane, when they take their boisterous black Labrador Kyle for a walk. That is about the most demanding part of the recipe, for once the nettles have been rinsed and chopped, the rest is child's play.

Nettle Soup

This nettle soup thickened with rolled oats, is most surprisingly good, for something so very simple and cheap (you would be hard pushed to spend more than 50p on it at the outside). The oats give it a wonderful, creamy consistency, while the nettles bring their particular green leafy taste. When she doesn't have time to make a proper vegetable stock, Fiona dilutes a few teaspoons of bought vegetable bouillon in water.

If you have never been introduced to the concept of nettles as food, then it will probably seem mighty strange, but fear not; once heat meets the stinging hairs of the nettle, they fall swiftly into submission, dispensing with their bite with barely a murmur. Think of nettles as a form of wild spinach that must be picked with gloved hands (washing up gloves are perfect) and you will begin to get the idea. For centuries, poor folk have relied on them in the early spring months, when other greens are few and far between. Nettles are immensely nutritious, and when picked have a divine sweet scent. Be sure to pluck just the top four or so leaves, which will be tender and full of flavour. The lower leaves, or those from more mature nettles, will be tough and fibrous. Rinse them thoroughly, and pick out any bits of grass and other unwanted leaves, then dry in a clean tea-towel before using.

fresh young nettle tops (see method)	
600 ml (1 pint) vegetable stock	
600 ml (1 pint) milk	
60g (2 oz) butter	
60g (2 oz) rolled oats	
1 tablespoon chopped parsley	
salt and pepper	

Chop the nettles. Pack them into a measuring jug until it is filled to the 600 ml (1 pint) level.

Bring the stock, milk and butter to the boil, then add the oats. Stir and bring back to the boil. Now tip in the nettles and stir. Season with salt and pepper, then reduce the heat down low, half cover the pan, and simmer very gently for 30 minutes. Stir in the parsley.

The next step is a matter of personal taste. The soup can be served just as it is, slightly knobbly but very creamy, but you may well prefer to liquidize the whole lot, for a smoother version. Whichever option you go for, taste the soup and adjust seasoning, then reheat if necessary before serving.

Fiona's Spinach and Feta Pie

Fiona's spinach and feta pie is a variation on that lovely Greek concoction, spanakopita, combining salty feta cheese with cottage cheese and Parmesan, spring onions and spinach. Frozen spinach is cheaper than fresh, and in a recipe like this it works very well. Filo pastry provides the crispest of crusts, and what isn't used straight away can be frozen for another day.

All four of the children like the spinach and feta pie, though they occasionally have had to tempt Moray into eating it by calling it 'silage pie' which amuses him no end. There's actually enough here to feed 6 people, but leftovers can be reheated in the oven for lunch next day, or popped into lunch-boxes when no-one is eating at home.

5 large sheets filo pastry, cut in half	
340g (12 oz) frozen spinach, cooked and thoroughly drained	
4 spring onions, finely chopped	
2 cloves garlic, crushed	
30g (1 oz) butter	
175g (6 oz) cottage cheese	
175g (6 oz) feta cheese, crumbled	
90g (3 oz) Parmesan cheese, freshly grated	
2 tablespoons chopped parsley	
4 eggs, lightly beaten	
sunflower oil for brushing	
1 tablespoon poppy seeds	
salt and pepper	

Pre-heat the oven to 190°C/375°F/Gas Mark 5. Cover the filo pastry with a sheet of greaseproof paper, then lay a damp tea-towel over that, to prevent it drying out.

Squeeze as much excess moisture as you can out of the spinach. Sauté the spring onions and garlic lightly in the butter. Mix with the cheeses, parsley and spinach, then beat in the eggs and season with salt and pepper.

Find an oven-proof dish that is more or less the same size as the halved sheets of filo (or very slightly smaller). One by one, take the first five pieces of filo, and brush lightly with oil. Lay on top of each other in the dish and spread the filling over the top. Brush the remaining 5 sheets lightly with oil, then use to cover the filling. Sprinkle the poppy seeds over the filo pastry.

Bake the pie for 35–45 minutes until golden brown and crisp.

Carrot and Raisin Salad

This is a straightforward grated carrot salad, dressed with a light vinaigrette and enlivened with a few raisins. Sometimes Fiona likes to add a sprinkling of pumpkin or sunflower seeds as well.

3 large carrots (around 300 g/10 oz), peeled and grated
30 g (1 oz) raisins
2 teaspoons white wine vinegar or lemon juice
¼ teaspoon Dijon mustard
2 tablespoons sunflower or olive oil
salt and pepper

Mix the carrots with the raisins. Whisk the vinegar with the mustard, salt and pepper, then gradually whisk in the oil. Pour over the carrots and raisins and turn to mix. Serve with the spinach and feta pie.

2

A *family* supper for six

Spaghetti, Meatballs and **No-Meatballs**

Roast Pineapple with **Butterscotch Sauce**

Feeding six hungry people for a fiver is no mean feat but when half of them are vegetarian and half are not that presents extra challenges. Oh, and one of them is a lively, strong-willed four year-old boy, who just happens to have become a great pal of mine. With young Moray in mind, I looked to my children's favourite dishes for inspiration. The answer was obvious – pasta with meatballs and tomato sauce, the one dish that my two never fail to gobble up with enthusiasm. However, Moray, like his mother and one of his sisters, does not eat meat, so for them I rolled up some no-meat balls, based on tofu but invigorated with black olives, sun-dried tomatoes, garlic and herbs.

As I was doing the shopping, I spotted a pile of pineapples going for a very reasonable price – they are often very good value in the spring, when other fruit is thin on the ground – so I grabbed one quickly to make a pudding that is handsome and fine tasting, but quick and easy.

Spaghetti, Meatballs and No-Meatballs

I don't quite understand the undeniable appeal of meatballs in tomato sauce on spaghetti but there is no doubt that they are a hit with adults and children alike. To be frank, they are among the few things I would really miss were I to turn vegetarian, not that that is very likely. But with both vegetarians and omnivores to feed, I wanted to create a meat-free alternative with some of the same appeal. These no-meatballs seemed to hit the spot with older vegetarians (and the meat-eaters, too), but young Moray flatly refused to even try them, though at least he did eat the spaghetti. You can't win them all ...

Both the meatballs and the no-meatballs can be prepared well in advance, as can the tomato sauce. Combine the balls with the sauce and reheat thoroughly once the spaghetti is boiling in its pan. When it comes to meatballs in tomato sauce, I have heretical leanings – I prefer to serve them with Cheddar rather than the more usual Parmesan.

600 g (1 lb 5 oz) spaghetti
100 g (3½ oz) Cheddar cheese, grated
sunflower or olive oil for frying
salt

For the meaty meatballs

1 thick slice of bread, crusts removed
a little milk
250 g (9 oz) minced beef or pork
1 garlic clove, finely chopped
1 tablespoon finely chopped marjoram
salt and pepper

For the no-meatballs

1 thick slice of bread, crusts removed
a little milk
200 g (7 oz) tofu, well-drained
2 garlic cloves, finely chopped
1 tablespoon finely chopped marjoram
45 g (1½ oz) black olives, stoned and finely chopped
2 teaspoons sun-dried tomato paste
a little flour
salt and pepper

For the tomato sauce

2 x 400 g (14 oz) tins of tomatoes
1 onion, chopped
1 carrot, diced small
1 celery stalk, diced small
2 tablespoons olive oil
3 garlic cloves, finely chopped
1 bouquet garni consisting of 2 sprigs of parsley, 2 sprigs of thyme, 2 bay leaves, tied together with string
2 teaspoons granulated or caster sugar
2 tablespoons tomato purée
salt and pepper

To make the meatballs, tear the bread up roughly, then soak in a little milk for 5 minutes. Squeeze out the milk and reserve. Put the bread into a bowl with all the remaining ingredients, and mix thoroughly with your hands, squeezing and squodging to distribute the bread evenly. Roll the mixture into balls, roughly the size of a small walnut. Fry in 1 tablespoon of oil, over a moderate heat, shaking the pan every now and then, until the balls are browned more or less on all sides, and cooked through. Drain on kitchen paper.

To make the no-meatballs, soften the bread in the milk as before, reserving the milk. Mash the tofu thoroughly with a fork, then mix with the bread and remaining ingredients, except the flour. Form into balls about the same size as the meatballs, dust lightly in flour, then fry in hot oil until browned on all sides. Drain on kitchen paper.

To make the sauce, begin by opening the tins of tomatoes, and chopping them in their tins with a sharp knife. Fry the onion, carrot and celery in the oil until patched with brown. Now add the garlic and fry for another minute or so. Add all the remaining ingredients to the pan, including the tomatoes and the reserved milk from the bread. Stir, then simmer gently for about 20 minutes until the sauce is fairly thick. Taste and adjust the seasoning.

Put half the sauce in second pan. Add the meatballs to the first pan, and simmer for 5 minutes or so (if the sauce becomes too thick, add a splash more milk or water). Simmer the second pan of sauce for a couple of minutes, then carefully add the no-meatballs, handling them delicately as they are softer and more prone to collapse than the meatballs. Simmer for 2–3 minutes to heat through.

Bring a large pan of well-salted water to the boil and add the spaghetti, easing it gently down into the water as it softens. Simmer until *al dente* (check the packet for approximate cooking times). Drain thoroughly and divide between 6 warm, shallow serving plates. Top each plate with a generous helping of tomato sauce and the relevant balls, finish with a scattering of cheese and serve immediately.

Roast Pineapple with Butterscotch Sauce

In early spring, pineapples are often to be had for low prices, so keep an eye out for special offers, or market stall bargains. Of course, if the pineapple is ripe, sweet and juicy (a ripe pineapple is one that smells fragrant and from which you can pluck the central spiky leaf with minimal effort), you may well want to serve it fresh and cool all on its own. Still, when pineapples are plentiful, or when the weather is a little less clement than one might wish for, hot, roasted pineapple makes a welcome, more dressy end to a meal. Preparation is speedy, the results delicious and unexpected.

1 small pineapple
30 g (1 oz) unsalted butter
60 g (2 oz) caster sugar
150 ml (¼ pint) double cream

Pre-heat the oven to 220°C/425°F/Gas Mark 6.

Peel the pineapple, leaving the top knot of leaves untouched and in place. Cut out the 'eyes', or at least the biggest ones if you are pushed for time, or patience. Cut the pineapple in half, from stem end right through the leaves. Wrap the leaves in silver foil to protect them from the heat of the oven.

Smear half of the butter thickly around a roasting tin that is just big enough to take the two pineapple halves, lying down. Lay the pineapple halves in the tin, cut sides up. Dredge the caster sugar over the cut sides, then dot with the remaining butter. Roast for 25 minutes.

Place the pineapple halves in a warm serving dish, cut side down, and keep warm while you make the sauce. Put the roasting tin on the hob and add a good splash of water. Bring up to the boil, stirring and scraping in all the caramelized, buttery juices from the base of the pan. When they have all dissolved (you may need to add a little extra water but don't overdo it – you only want just enough to dissolve the goo on the tin), stir in the cream. Bring up to the boil, and simmer for 1–2 minutes until slightly thickened. Pour into a bowl or jug. Remove the foil coats from the pineapple leaves, and serve the pineapple immediately. Slice it at the table and pass the sauce around separately.

Following page
(From left to right):
Roast Pineapple with
Butterscotch Sauce;
Spaghetti, Meatballs
and No-Meatballs

Menu for a *musical* evening (for four)

Pearl Barley Risotto with **Mushrooms**

Buttered Lettuce with **Lemon** and **Cumin**

Blood Orange Torta

As well as playing in the orchestra, Fiona and Stephen also play in an informal quartet with two friends, Peter on cello and Gerry on violin. They come together mainly for the love of it, with the occasional gig at charity performances, weddings and other parties. They practise in the front room of Fiona and Stephen's house, and I tell you there are few things more congenial to a cook than rustling up supper with strains of Mozart wafting through the house, from your very own live quartet.

Springtime it may have been but the weather outside was perfectly vile, with rain pelting down and wind gusting icily. What better to keep out the chills than a risotto, creamy and comforting, and intensely flavoured? The trouble is, of course, that proper risotto rice does not come cheap, and I wanted to be able to offer up some sort of pudding as well as perhaps a small side dish. The answer is obvious: don't use rice at all. Over the past few years, a new form of risotto made with pearl barley – an *orzotto* – has become fashionable both in Italy and in smart restaurants in the UK. The joy of it is that pearl barley is blissfully cheap, which means that even on our very restricted allowance we can still afford a few luxuries like dried porcini mushrooms and Parmesan. Problem solved.

For the pudding, I turned to an old favourite of mine, based on a Portuguese recipe. It is, essentially, an orange custard Swiss roll, with the milk or cream replaced by freshly squeezed fruit juice. Since it is very rich, a little goes a long way. The recipe actually makes enough to feed six people, so there will be some left over for another meal. Just as well, since, I have to admit, the cost of this menu would otherwise sneak over the £5 limit by some 30 pence.

Making music obviously whets the appetite. As the last notes of the Oboe Quartet in F died away, stomachs rumbled and the quartet sat down eagerly to eat. As first the *orzotto* and buttered lettuce, then the pudding, were wolfed down, Gerry regaled us with a string of viola player jokes. Viola players, they explained, are the Irishmen of the orchestra, the butt of all jokes. Our very own viola player, Fiona, took it all in customary good spirit. She's used to it, I guess.

Pearl Barley and Mushroom Risotto

The expression on Fiona's face was hard to fathom as she tried a mouthful of this pearl barley risotto. Then suddenly she was all smiles. It turned out that as a child she had loathed the pearl barley that floated in bowls of Scotch broth. 'I always thought it had the texture of a slug,' she declared, which explained her expression. That mouthful of *orzotto* had been her first taste of pearl barley in over 30 years, and she loved it!

This has certainly become one of my hot-favourite new dishes for cool weather. It has all the flavour of a true risotto, but the big advantage is that it doesn't have to be stirred constantly, which means that you can get on with other things as it cooks. The disadvantage (why is there almost always at least one?) is that you do have to remember to soak the pearl barley overnight, and then to pre-cook it for 20 minutes. Still, that's not really too onerous a burden for something as good as this.

Porcini is the Italian for a cep or boletus mushroom, and although the dried ones seem phenomenally expensive, a mere half an ounce (15 g) adds a big, big helping hand to the plainer button mushrooms.

340 g (12 oz) pearl barley, soaked overnight, then drained
15 g (½ oz) dried porcini
600 ml (1 pint) chicken or vegetable stock
1 onion, chopped
1 tablespoon sunflower oil
45 g (1½ oz) butter
2 garlic cloves, chopped
125 g (4½ oz) button mushrooms, sliced
60 ml (2 fl oz) sweet sherry or Marsala
30 g (1 oz) Parmesan cheese, freshly grated
2 tablespoons finely chopped fresh parsley
salt and pepper

Tip the barley into a pan of lightly salted boiling water and simmer for 20 minutes. Meanwhile, pour enough hot water over the dried porcini to cover and then leave to soak for 20 minutes. Pick out the pieces of mushroom and chop roughly. Let the soaking liquid settle, then carefully pour it out of the bowl into a saucepan, leaving the grit behind. Add the stock and bring up to the boil.

Cook the onion gently in the sunflower oil and 15 g (½ oz) of the butter in a roomy, deep frying pan, or wide, shallow saucepan. When it is tender, add the garlic, porcini and sliced button mushrooms. Fry for about 4 minutes, until the mushrooms have softened. Now tip in the barley, stir briefly, then pour in the sherry or Marsala. Stir for about 2 minutes, until the liquid has virtually evaporated. Now add the boiling stock, all in one fell swoop, season and leave to simmer gently for about 15–20 minutes until most of the liquid has been absorbed and the barley is tender. Stir in the remaining butter, plus the Parmesan and parsley, then taste and adjust seasoning. Serve immediately.

Following page
(From left to right):
Buttered Lettuce with
Cumin and Lemon; Blood
Orange Iorta; Pearl Barley
and Mushroom Risotto

Buttered Lettuce with Cumin and Lemon

A small touch of green, with the sharpness of lemon, is welcome alongside the richness of the pearl barley risotto. When I was casting around for something fresh and sprightly that would cost no more than a mere 25p, my eyes lit upon the tender form of a floppy round lettuce – the stuff of so many desperately dull salads. This dish, though, is anything but dull. A touch of warmth brings out the best in the greenery, aided and abetted by a squeeze or two of lemon juice, and the aromatic flavour of fried cumin seeds. If you are feeling wildly extravagant, you might even consider doubling the quantities, to create larger helpings, but, of course, you will be exceeding the budget by a handful of pennies.

½ round lettuce
15 g (½ oz) butter
1 level teaspoon cumin seeds
a couple of squeezes of lemon juice
salt and pepper

Cut the lettuce into wide ribbons. Just before serving heat the butter until it foams. Add the cumin seeds and fry for about 30 seconds. Turn off the heat and add the lemon juice, salt and pepper. Stir, then add the lettuce. Toss to mix, then serve absolutely and unequivocally immediately, before the lettuce wilts too severely.

Orange Torta

To me, a torta implies some sort of cake or tart, probably round in shape. Well, this one is round, it's true, but not as you might imagine. The mixture of juice, sugar and eggs is baked in a Swiss roll tin, then rolled up just like ... well, a Swiss roll. Not that it tastes anything remotely like a Swiss Roll. This is something remarkably special, with its soft, slightly sticky, jelly-like texture and its perfume of fresh orange.

I think it is nicest made with freshly squeezed blood orange juice, but when we were in Glasgow the local supermarket had only two left, so we compromised by using ordinary sweet oranges in the torta itself and slicing the precious blood oranges (often sold as ruby red oranges) to serve with it. The combination looked most striking. In January you can experiment with making the torta from the juice of Seville oranges, but stick with ordinary sweet oranges or clementines to slice and serve with it.

If you don't have quite the right-sized Swiss roll tin (or roasting tin, which works just as well), use one that is a little smaller. A larger one will not do – there just isn't enough mixture to fill it.

4 large eggs
finely grated zest and juice of 3 blood oranges or 3 small sweet oranges
1½ tablespoons cornflour
finely grated zest and juice of ½ lemon
225 g (8 oz) caster sugar, plus extra for sprinkling
a little butter and flour, for preparing the tin

To serve
2 blood oranges or sweet oranges

Preheat the oven to 180°C/350°F/Gas Mark 4.

Line the base of a 20 cm x 30 cm (8 x 12 inch) Swiss roll tin with non-stick baking parchment. Butter and flour the sides. Beat the eggs lightly. Mix a tablespoon of the orange juice into the cornflour, and then a second tablespoon to form a smooth runny cream, then whisk lightly into the eggs. Now add the remaining orange juice, the lemon juice and the sugar. Whisk for about 2 minutes with an electric whisk, until the mixture has thickened and the sugar has dissolved, then pour the mixture into the tin and bake for 15–20 minutes, until just firm.

Meanwhile, lay a clean teatowel on a work surface and sprinkle heavily with caster sugar. As soon as the roll is cooked, run a thin-bladed knife around the edge, then take a deep breath and quickly invert it on to the sugared towel. Remove the tin, then carefully ease off the baking parchment, using a knife to unstick any tiresome, clingy patches. Trim the edges and roll up snugly, starting from one of the narrow ends, using the towel to guide and cajole the roll into place. Leave to cool, still wrapped in the towel. Chill for 3–4 hours.

Meanwhile, peel the oranges to the flesh, and slice into rounds. Chill lightly. To serve, unwrap the roll, cut into slices, and arrange on a serving plate, alternating with slices of fresh orange.

4

The *call of the-wild* menu for four

Nettle and **Tomato Bredy** with **Wild Garlic Mash**

Greek Honey Syrup Cake

Mid-spring is the time to start raiding the wild larder. Everything is suddenly sprouting forth, green and vigorous and joyful. It may be too early for summer vegetables and fruit, but there is plenty going on in the hedgerows and woods, and even in most back gardens. Nettles are the first thing to go for. They are recognised by one and all (but take care not to pick dead nettles, which don't sting), and they are surprisingly good to eat. Not raw, obviously, but lightly cooked they taste vaguely spinachy, without that tooth-furring quality that spinach sometimes has. I can't deny that nettle dishes are spiced by the pleasure of getting a spot of revenge into the bargain – it's very comforting to be getting one's own back on pesky weeds.

If you like bitter leaves, then pick young spring dandelions, or to reduce the bitterness, cover young plants with an upturned flowerpot, then cover the draining hole with a stone so that no light can enter. Leave for a week or so, then uncover to reveal pale yellow, emaciated leaves, which have spent so much time searching for the light that they have become milder in taste. Lovely in salads.

Wild garlic produces one of the prettiest of springtime flowers, with its delicate white petals, but it takes a little more searching out than nettles and dandelions. Once you've found a stand of wild garlic, however, it will serve you well year after year, as long as you do not disturb the bulbs. (For more ideas on how to cook wild garlic, glance at a copy of my book, *Sophie Grigson's Herbs*).

In this menu, the nettles appear in a main course stew, made with the cheapest cut of lamb but drawing out all the flavour of its bone. Wild garlic comes with it, beaten into a light, buttery mash and, to cap it all, there is a sweet finale of a sticky, syrup-soaked cake – nothing wild in that, but it rounds the whole meal off in a most satisfying way.

Nettle and Tomato Bredy

A bredy is a Cape Malay stew from South Africa. Back in the seventeenth and eighteenth centuries Malaysians were brought over to South Africa to work for white masters, and with them came their style of cooking which they adapted to the produce of this new land. The result is Cape Malay cooking, richly flavoured, often spicy, often combining savoury and sweet as in this stew.

A bredy is usually made with lamb or mutton, with plenty of onions for body and sweetness, all brought together with the particular vegetable that is most widely available at the time of cooking. Tomato bredy is an old favourite of mine, but spinach bredy is very good, too. Why not, then, in this season of young spring nettles, combine them with tomatoes. Of course, tomatoes are still way out of season, but tinned tomatoes are inexpensive and marvellous for cooking. If you can't hack the thought of picking nettles, then you can substitute either frozen spinach (the same quantity) or better still, fresh spinach (about half as much again).

For notes on picking and preparing nettles, turn to page 129.

1 kilo (2¼ lb) onions, sliced
4 tablespoons sunflower or vegetable oil
900 g (2 lb) scrag end or neck of lamb, chopped into thick slices
seasoned flour
4 garlic cloves, chopped
1–2 fresh red chillies, deseeded and thinly sliced
4 bay leaves
2 teaspoons ground cinnamon
2 tablespoons dark muscovado sugar
2 x 400 g (14 oz) tins of tomatoes, chopped in their tins
200 g (7 oz) young nettle tops, rinsed and roughly chopped
salt and pepper

Pre-heat the oven to 150°C/300°F/Gas Mark 2. Fry the onions gently in 2 tablespoons of the oil in a frying pan, until golden and tender – this will take some 15–20 minutes, which gives you plenty of time to chop the garlic and chillies. Scoop the onions out into a flame-proof casserole. Add the remaining oil to the frying pan. Dust the pieces of lamb with seasoned flour, then fry briskly in the oil to brown – you'll probably have to do this in two or even three batches. Put the browned meat into the casserole. When all the meat has been browned, place the casserole over the heat, and add the garlic, chillies, bay leaves, cinnamon and sugar. Stir about for 2–3 minutes to mix all the ingredients thoroughly.

Next tip in the tomatoes and add enough water to cover the meat. Season with salt and pepper and bring up to the boil. Transfer to the oven and leave to cook gently for 2 hours.

Now is the moment of glory for those nettles. Pull on the rubber gloves for the last time and carefully cram the nettles into the casserole. Cover tightly and continue cooking for 10 minutes, by which time they will have begun to soften. Stir them into the bredy and return to the oven, again three-quarters covered, for another 30 minutes–1 hour, until the meat is so tender that it is falling off the bone.

Serve with wild garlic mash (see opposite) or plain mash or rice.

Wild Garlic Mash

This is really a springtime play on the Irish theme of mash with greens, but instead of the spring onions or cabbage, I've used the gloriously pongy wild garlic that comes absolutely free at this time of year. If you have ever wandered through a wood at bluebell time and remarked on the pervasive reek of garlic, and perhaps noticed beautiful white flowers on slender stems, surrounded by leaves that could almost be those of a hyacinth, or tulip, then you have been amongst wild garlic. It grows in woods and damp hedgerows (there's a lovely vigorous patch just on the edge of the village road, five minutes' walk from our house). The tender leaves poke their heads up in March, and come into flower in late April or May. Only pick it if you are sure you know what it is, and always double check that it does indeed carry a powerful scent of garlic. When young and tender, the leaves, shredded, are great in salads. By the time the flowers appear, they are better lightly cooked.

1 kg (2¼ lb) floury main-crop potatoes	
2 large handfuls (about 150 g/5 oz) wild garlic leaves	
45 g (1½ oz) butter	
150 ml–300 ml (¼–½ fl oz) hot milk	
salt	

Either bake the potatoes or cook in the microwave. If you must boil them, leave them whole and cook in their skins so that they don't absorb too much water. While they cook, rinse the garlic leaves, dry as well as you can, then shred finely.

When the potatoes are done, and while they are still hot, if possible, scoop out the flesh (or skin them, if boiled) into a saucepan. Add half the butter, season with salt, and then mash or beat the potatoes over a moderate heat (a hand-held electric whisk does the job most efficiently, but don't go on for too long or you'll end up with a

gluey texture), gradually adding enough hot milk to give the kind of consistency you prefer; I like mashed potatoes verging on runny, but not everyone does.

Melt the remaining butter in a frying pan over a moderate heat and sauté the wild garlic in it very briefly until wilted. Stir into the steaming-hot mash. Taste and adjust the seasoning, then serve with the stew.

Greek Honey Syrup Cake

This kind of syrup-soaked cake makes a superb pudding, served perhaps with spoonfuls of rich Greek yoghurt, though that will take you through the £5 barrier, I'm afraid. It keeps very well, and in fact is better eaten the day after it is made. There is enough here to feed a party of four twice over, so save the rest for teatime.

3 eggs	
110 g (4 oz) caster sugar	
100 ml (4 fl oz) sunflower oil	
½ tablespoon brandy (optional)	
225 g (8 oz) semolina	
1½ teaspoons baking powder	
45 g (1½ oz) whole, blanched almonds, split in half	

For the syrup	
150 g (5 oz) caster sugar	
2 tablespoons honey	
2 cloves	
250 ml (8 fl oz) water	

Pre-heat the oven to 190°C/375°F/Gas Mark 5.

Make the syrup first, so that it has time to cool. Put all the ingredients into a saucepan and stir over a moderate heat until the sugar has dissolved. Bring up to the boil and simmer for 10 minutes, then leave to cool.

Line the base of a 23 cm (9 inch) springform cake tin with non-stick baking parchment. Oil the sides. Whisk the eggs with the caster sugar until thick and foamy. Whisk in the oil and the brandy if using. Mix the semolina with the baking powder and fold into the batter. Pour into the prepared tin. Arrange the halved almonds on top. Bake for about 30–40 minutes until the cake is firm to the touch and a skewer inserted into the centre comes out clean.

Don't unmould the cake, but while it is still hot, pierce holes all over it with the skewer, then pour over the cold syrup. Leave to cool, then cut into wedges and serve.

5

Annabel's *spring* menu for four

Fish Soup with **Fennel Seeds** and **Chives**

Chicken Liver and **Spinach Pancakes**

I sat moaning to my old friend and colleague, Annabel (she's the one who has slaved behind the scenes to prepare the food for the television programmes) about how difficult it is to come up with interesting spring menus once you have used up your quota of asparagus and rhubarb. It's a funny time of year for food. There are cheery daffodils and frolicking spring lambs aplenty, but certainly in the early part of the season there's really not much in the way of interesting produce to be had, especially when you are working on a tight budget. A leg of spring lamb is out of the question, though you might get away with a chunk of scrag end for a stew. Spring greens and cabbages are plentiful, but man or woman cannot live on cabbages alone. Shall I go on? No! cried Annabel. And to make doubly sure that I didn't warble on about it any longer, she volunteered to lighten my load by coming up with a spring menu of her own, and this is it.

Thanks, Annabel, but you've got to admit that I do have a point …

Incidentally, Annabel being of a thrifty nature, these two dishes came in at well under a fiver, leaving just enough dosh for a good helping of veg on the side – those plentiful spring greens, maybe, finely shredded and stir-fried with a touch of garlic, or a heap of grated carrot, cooked through gently in a little butter and enlivened with a dash of lemon juice.

Fish Soup with Fennel Seeds and Chives

It's amazing what you can do with a piece of cheap coley. Frankly, it's not one of the ocean's greatest treasures, but to my mind it is the soft, woolly texture that lets it down. The flavour itself is fine. So the trick with coley is to use it in ways that make the texture immaterial, and this is an ideal example. The fish is finely diced so that it can impart all its flavour to the soup, and indeed almost melts down into it. Add fennel seeds, chives and paprika, too, and you have an astonishingly pleasant soup for very minor outlay.

30 g (1 oz) butter
½ teaspoon fennel seeds
225 g (8 oz) skinned coley fillet, finely diced
4 tablespoons plain flour
½ teaspoon paprika
600 ml (1 pint) milk
600 ml (1 pint) water
juice of ½ lemon
1 tablespoon chopped fresh chives
salt and pepper

Melt the butter in a large saucepan. When it is foaming, throw in the fennel seeds and fry gently for about 1 minute. Add the coley and stir. Sprinkle over the flour and half the paprika. Stir for about 30 seconds, then gradually add the milk, stirring continuously, and finally the water. Bring up to the boil, stirring frequently, then reduce the heat and simmer for 10–15 minutes. Draw off the heat, stir in the lemon juice, salt and pepper and chopped chives, then taste and adjust the seasoning. Pour into a warmed soup tureen or individual bowls. Dust the surface of the soup with the remaining paprika and serve.

Chicken Liver and Spinach Pancakes

How often do you make pancakes? If the answer is once a year on Pancake Day, if at all, then shame on you. You could almost describe pancakes as a form of pasta, for their soft, pliable texture and mild but distinctive taste mean that they are a great vehicle for all kinds of flavours, from the very simple, such as lemon juice and sugar, to the heady gastronomic heights of crêpes Suzette. They work well, too, with all manner of savoury food, and this is what we have here. A filling of chicken livers and spinach, the whole covered in a speckled green sauce. If you want to gild this humble lily, and you don't mind a touch of minor extravagance, you could contrive a crisp, cheesy topping by sprinkling a mixture of breadcrumbs and grated Parmesan over the top, then dotting it with butter, before baking, uncovered, for the full half hour until browned.

Note that the quantity of spinach given in the filling is actually to be divided between filling and sauce. The dish can be prepared entirely in advance, then reheated and browned in the oven at your convenience.

For the pancakes

110 g (4 oz) plain flour
¼ teaspoon salt
1 egg
300 ml (½ pint) milk
2 tablespoons sunflower oil

continued on page 148

Following page
(From left to right):
Chicken Liver and Spinach
Pancakes; Fish Soup with
Fennel Seeds and Chives

continued from page 145

For the filling

30 g (1 oz) butter

1 onion, chopped

2 garlic cloves, crushed

4 rashers of unsmoked back bacon, diced

450 g (1 lb) chicken livers, defrosted if frozen, chopped

500 g (1 lb 2 oz) frozen chopped spinach, cooked and thoroughly drained

2 tablespoons crème fraîche

salt and pepper

For the sauce

30 g (1 oz) butter

30 g (1 oz) plain flour

300 ml (½ pint) milk

freshly grated nutmeg

salt and pepper

First make the pancake batter. Sift the flour and salt into a bowl, make a well in the centre and add the egg and half the milk. Start whisking them into the flour, gradually adding the rest of the milk, to form a smooth batter. Cover and leave to stand for 30 minutes while you make the filling.

For the filling, begin by melting the butter in a wide frying pan. Fry the onion and garlic gently in the butter until soft. Add the bacon and fry for 5 minutes. Add the chopped livers and stir until lightly browned – another 4–5 minutes. Set aside half the spinach for the sauce, then stir the other half and the crème fraîche into the chicken livers. Season the filling with salt and pepper, then draw the pan off the heat.

Just before cooking the pancakes, stir 1 tablespoon of the oil into the batter. Brush a 25 cm (10 inch) frying pan with a little of the remaining oil. Heat over a moderate heat, then pour in enough batter just to cover the base of the pan, tipping and tilting the pan so that it spreads evenly. Cook until the underneath is lightly patched with brown, then turn over and cook the other side until also patched with brown. Make 8 pancakes altogether.

Divide the filling between the pancakes, spreading it down the centre of each one, then rolling the pancake up around it. Snuggle the pancakes into a closely fitting shallow dish.

Pre-heat the oven to 190°C/375°F/Gas Mark 5.

To make the sauce, melt the butter in a saucepan, then add the flour and stir over a low heat for about 1 minute. Draw off the heat and gradually add the milk, stirring it in thoroughly with each addition, until you have a smooth sauce. Bring up to the boil, then reduce the heat and simmer gently for a good 5 minutes to cook out the flavour of raw flour. Stir in the reserved chopped spinach and then season with nutmeg, salt and pepper. Pour evenly over the pancakes.

If the ingredients are all still hot, just heat through in the oven for 10–15 minutes. If you are reheating from cold, cover with foil and bake for 30 minutes.

6

Two-times two – an asparagus and rhubarb *double bill* for four

Two-times-two *mark one*

Scrambled Eggs with **Asparagus Tips** and **Horseradish**

Chicken and **Tarragon Patties** with **Onion Marmalade**

Rhubarb and **Orange Jelly** with **Cardamom**

· Following page (From left to right): Scrambled Eggs with Asparagus Tips and Horseradish; Chicken and Tarragon Patties with Onion Marmalade; Rhubarb and Orange Jelly with Cardamom

This double bill celebrates two of late spring's most welcome arrivals, fine British asparagus and garden rhubarb. Every year I anticipate the sighting of the first slender stems of home-grown asparagus with impatience. More than anything else, they signal the start of the lighter, brighter foods to come over the summer months.

But summer is still on the horizon, and we haven't yet reached that wonderful period of plenty and freshness and warmth. There's precious little fresh fruit to be had, apart from unseasonal imports. Rhubarb gallops in to fill the breach; not the bright-pink forced rhubarb of winter but the irrepressible, prolific, thrusting stems of garden rhubarb – at their very best, still tender and relatively mild. If there's a rhubarb plant in your garden you'll know how easily it grows. If you don't, then you'll find that it costs very little, maybe nothing at all if you can beg some from a gardener – there's always more than enough to go round.

To make the most of your rhubarb and asparagus, harness the two together and use every last bit to stretch the costs over two meals. Both financially and practically, these menus go hand in hand – symbiotic, you might say – each using up the byproducts of the other.

7

Two-times-two *mark two*

Velouté d'Asperges

Grilled Mackerel Fillets with **Feisty Rhubarb Relish**

Elderflower Fritters with **Vanilla Ruby Sauce**

Menu 6

Scrambled Eggs with Asparagus Tips and Horseradish

Asparagus and eggs are perfect partners, and this simple dish of asparagus stirred into softly scrambled eggs with a dash of horseradish is a real springtime treat. Use only the choice, tender tips for this starter and save the tougher lower part to make the soup for the second menu.

If you have a handy source of cheap asparagus near where you live (I'm lucky enough to have a pick-your-own asparagus farm a few miles away from my house), then make the most of it while the season lasts. One of my other favourite asparagus and egg combinations, just as simple as this one, is lightly cooked asparagus with soft-boiled eggs – just dip the green spears into the runny yolks as if they were Marmite soldiers. And if you want to get a bit more fancy, try the Milanese dish of steamed asparagus served with eggs fried in olive oil and a generous grating of fresh Parmesan.

450 g (1 lb) asparagus
6 eggs
30 g (1 oz) butter
2–3 teaspoons creamed horseradish
salt and pepper

Cut the upper 5 cm (2 inches) of tip from the asparagus and set the lower part of the stems aside to make soup (see page 154). Simmer the tips in salted water for 3–6 minutes, depending on how soft you like them. Drain thoroughly and keep warm, or reheat in a little extra butter when needed.

Beat the eggs with some salt and pepper. Melt the butter in a saucepan over a moderate heat, then tip in the eggs. Reduce the heat down very low and stir continuously until the eggs thicken to form soft, creamy curds – not runny, but certainly not set to a miserable mass of polystyrene clumps. Stir in the horseradish and asparagus and serve immediately.

Chicken and Tarragon Patties with Onion Marmalade

These chicken and tarragon patties (or burgers if you prefer) have proved an enormous success in our household. We all love them, parents and children alike. My five-year-old, who usually objects lock, stock and barrel to anything with green herbs in it, tucks into these ravenously, despite the tarragon. The rest of us greet the tarragon with unabashed enthusiasm.

A whole chicken is a real bargain. A bit of easy butchering, which will take only a few minutes of your time, transforms the bird into a pair of prime boneless chicken breasts, two meaty legs, and a carcass ready for making your own stock – so much nicer than stock cubes. If you really can't stand the thought of hacking up a chicken yourself, then 500 g (1 lb 2 oz) minced chicken is what you will need to make the patties, though sadly you won't be able to make the stock, unless you can blag a few chicken bones from your butcher.

The sweet-sharp onion marmalade can be made a day or more ahead of time, as it keeps well, covered, in the fridge. The patties have a shorter shelf-life, but they can still be put together several hours in advance and stored in the fridge. Bring them back to room temperature before cooking.

1 whole chicken (see method)
60 g (2 oz) fresh breadcrumbs
leaves from 2 sprigs of tarragon, finely chopped
1 teaspoon Dijon mustard
1 egg, beaten
sunflower oil for frying
salt and pepper

For the onion marmalade

2 tablespoons sunflower oil
500 g (1 lb 2 oz) onions, thinly sliced
½ teaspoon ground cinnamon
60 g (2 oz) caster sugar
2 tablespoons red wine vinegar

To make the marmalade, begin by heating the oil in a wide saucepan, then add the onions and cinnamon. Stir about to coat more or less in oil, then cover and cook very gently over a low heat for 20 minutes, until soft. Uncover and cook for another 10 minutes or so to drive off the liquid and begin to colour the onions. Now add the sugar, vinegar and a little salt. Cook for a further 10 minutes or so, stirring frequently, until dark and sticky. Leave to cool.

To make the patties, cut the legs and breasts off the chicken, reserving the carcass for stock (see page 154). Skin all the portions, and add the skin to the carcass. Strip as much meat as you can from the legs and then put the bones on the stock pile. If you have a mincer, the next step is a doddle. Just cut the meat up into smallish pieces and pass through the mincer. Otherwise, cut the meat up into dice, then process in brief bursts in a food processor, scraping down the sides in between bursts. Don't be tempted to leave the motor running or you will end up with an overprocessed chicken paste. If you don't own a food processor, then sharpen your best knife and chop the chicken meat very, very finely. Mix with the breadcrumbs, tarragon, mustard, salt and pepper, using your hands to mulch it all together thoroughly. Add just enough beaten egg to bind the mixture without making it sloppy. Divide into 4 portions. Wash your hands, then flour them lightly and form each chicken portion into a round patty about 1 cm (½ inch) thick. Store in the fridge, covered and well away from other food.

To cook, heat a little sunflower oil in a heavy-based frying pan until hazy. Lay the patties in the pan and leave, without moving, for about 4 minutes, by which time they should have formed a nice crust underneath. Turn them over and cook the other side, until they are cooked through. Serve immediately with the onion marmalade.

Rhubarb and Orange Jelly with Cardamom

I was a late starter when it comes to rhubarb. Both my parents loathed the stuff, having been force-fed badly cooked stewed rhubarb as children, so it was only when I started to cook for myself, as a student, that I discovered how delicious it can be, once you shed the prejudice. One of the things I noticed fairly swiftly was that rhubarb produces a great deal of juice when cooked, and that the juice tastes as good as the rhubarb itself, if not better. These jellies are made from that juice and are so good that they will soften the heart of the most ardent rhubarb hater. I suspect that even my mother and father would have downed them with relish. Talking of which, save the rhubarb itself to make the relish to accompany the mackerel in the following menu.

650 g (1½ lb) garden rhubarb, leaves cut off
juice of 2 oranges
340 g (12 oz) caster sugar
4 sheets of leaf gelatine
3 cardamom pods

Pre-heat the oven to 180°C/350°F/Gas Mark 4.

Cut the rhubarb into 2.5 cm (1 inch) lengths and place in an ovenproof dish with the orange juice and sugar. Cover (with foil if there is no acceptable lid) and leave in the oven for about 25–30 minutes, until the rhubarb is just tender but still firm enough to hold its shape. Drain off the liquid and measure out 600 ml (1 pint) of it. If you don't have quite enough, make up the quantity with a little extra orange juice.

Half fill a roasting tin with cold water and lay the sheets of gelatine in it to soak for a few minutes. Meanwhile, slit open the cardamom pods and extract the seeds. Crush them as finely as you can in a mortar and pestle or in a sturdy bowl with the end of a rolling pin. Put the liquid into a pan with the crushed cardamom seeds. Bring to just under the boil, turn the heat way down low, and let the mixture infuse gently for 10 minutes. If the heat won't go down low enough to take the juice off the boil, draw the pan off the heat, cover and leave for 10 minutes, then reheat gently. One by one, take the gelatine leaves out of the cold water, slough off excess water and stir the gelatine into the hot juice. Strain the juice into 4 wine glasses. Leave to cool, then transfer to the fridge to set.

Menu 7
Velouté d'Asperges

Velouté d'asperges is nothing more than asparagus soup, but asparagus soup is such a delightful creation that it deserves a fancy name. It is truly a triumph of good housekeeping, for the most important elements in it are leftovers: the tough lower stems of the asparagus that are too fibrous to eat as they are, and the stock made from the chicken carcass.

1 onion, chopped
30 g (1 oz) butter
450 g (1 lb) potatoes, peeled and diced
the remainder of the asparagus used for the scrambled eggs (see page 152), roughly chopped
600 ml (1 pint) chicken stock (see below)
1 bay leaf
300 ml (½ pint) milk
dash of lemon juice
salt and pepper

Cook the onion in the butter until softened, then add the diced potato and the asparagus. Stir to coat in the butter, then cover and sweat over a very low heat for 10 minutes. Now add the chicken stock, bay leaf, salt and pepper and bring up to the boil. Simmer gently for about 15 minutes until the vegetables are very tender. Cool slightly, remove the bay leaf, then liquidize the soup until smooth. Rub through a sieve to remove any asparagus strings, then stir in the milk. Reheat, add a dash of lemon juice to bring out the flavours, then adjust the seasoning and serve.

Chicken Stock

Never waste chicken bones. Once you have stripped off the flesh of the chicken for the patties in the previous menu, put the carcass into a large pan straight away, add a few aromatics and plenty of water and leave it to bubble away, forming a deeply savoury stock that will be the basis, in this instance, of a classy asparagus soup.

This list of vegetables and herbs is the standard, ideal collection for adding depths to stocks, but don't panic if you don't have all of them to hand. If you have to do without a leek, say, it won't be the end of the world.

Makes about 1.75 litres (3 pints)

carcass and skin of 1 chicken
1 onion, quartered
1 carrot, quartered
1 leek or 3 spring onions, roughly chopped
1 bay leaf
1 sprig of parsley
1 sprig of thyme
6 peppercorns
3 litres (5¼ pints) water

Put all the ingredients into a large saucepan, bring up to the boil and simmer slowly for about 3 hours, topping up the water level with hot water as it drops. Strain through a sieve.

If you have a microwave, put all the stock ingredients, except the water, into the largest microwaveable bowl you have and pour over enough boiling water to cover. Microwave on full power for 30 minutes, then leave for 25 minutes before straining.

Grilled Mackerel Fillets with Feisty Rhubarb Relish

The rich flesh of mackerel begs a sharp, fruity accompaniment. Gooseberry sauce is one of the traditional, perfectly judged accompaniments, and less well known but equally good is rhubarb sauce. In this recipe I've updated the idea by turning the cooked rhubarb left over from the jellies in the previous menu into a zippy relish to serve with grilled mackerel fillets.

Both the relish and the mackerel fillets can be prepared in advance, so all you have to do before eating is grill the fillets for a few minutes.

4 small or 2 large mackerel (around 1 kg/2¼ lb total weight), filleted

2 garlic cloves, sliced

1 tablespoon chopped fresh parsley

grated zest and juice of ½ lemon

1 tablespoon olive oil

salt and pepper

For the relish

225 g (8 oz) of the cooked rhubarb left over from the Rhubarb and Orange Jelly with Cardamom (see page 153), diced

1 red chilli, deseeded and very finely chopped

2 spring onions, thinly sliced

2 tablespoons chopped fresh coriander

Put the mackerel fillets in a shallow dish. Pound the garlic, parsley and lemon zest together in a mortar (or use a sturdy bowl and the end of the rolling pin), gradually working in the lemon juice and olive oil and seasoning with salt and pepper. Smear this mixture over the mackerel fillets, then leave to marinate for at least half an hour.

To make the relish, mix all the ingredients together and season to taste.

Pre-heat the grill thoroughly and line the grill rack with silver foil, so that the fillets don't collapse through the bars. Lay the mackerel skin-side up on the foil and grill close to the heat until the skin is browned (about 5–8 minutes), by which time the mackerel should be cooked through. Serve with the relish.

rhubarb

Elderflower Fritters with Vanilla Ruby Sauce

With economy riding high in mind, there can be few better late-spring puddings than elderflower fritters. The elderflowers themselves are free for the picking, and can be found in towns and countryside right across the land. Pick them as far away as possible from the heavy fumes of busy roads, and take only those that have just opened (check by giving the creamy white umbels of flowers a gentle shake – if white petals rain down, it is definitely too far gone). If you have any doubts about what you are picking, leave them alone until you can find someone to tell you for sure whether they really are elderflowers. They aren't difficult to identify, but there's no point in taking risks.

If you can't take the thought of any more rhubarb, then serve them with nothing more fancy than a dusting of sugar and a squeeze of lemon juice. However, I make no apologies for including rhubarb twice over in this menu. The vanilla ruby sauce makes the most superb sweet-sharp accompaniment to the fritters, and since it produces something utterly unlike the relish of the preceding recipe I don't think anyone is likely to suffer from rhubarb overkill.

2 tablespoons sunflower oil
15 g (½ oz) butter
8 fine heads of elderflowers
a little caster sugar, to serve

For the sauce

45 g (1½ oz) caster sugar
150 ml (¼ pint) water
225 g (8 oz) of the cooked rhubarb left over from the Rhubarb and Orange Jelly with Cardamom (see page 154)
½ teaspoon vanilla essence

For the batter

150 g (5 oz) plain flour
a pinch of salt
1 egg, separated
150 ml (¼ pint) milk
150 ml (¼ pint) fizzy mineral water
1 tablespoon melted butter

To make the sauce, put the sugar and water into a pan and heat over a moderate heat, stirring until the sugar has dissolved. Add the rhubarb and bring up to the boil. Simmer for 1 minute, then draw off the heat and add the vanilla essence. Cool slightly, then liquidize until smooth. Serve the sauce cold, warm or hot.

To make the batter, sift the flour and salt into a bowl, make a well in the centre and add the egg yolk and the milk. Beat together, gradually drawing in the flour and slowly adding the fizzy water, until you have a smooth batter with the consistency of runny double cream. If you have the time to spare, let the batter stand for half an hour or so before using.

When you are nearly ready for pudding, mix the melted butter into the batter. Whisk the egg white until it forms soft peaks, then fold it into the batter. Heat the sunflower oil and butter in a wide frying pan until the butter is foaming. One by one (you'll probably have to cook them in batches unless you have 2 pans on the go at once), take the first 4 elderflower heads by the stalk, dip the flowers into the batter, then place, batter-covered flowers downwards, in the fat in the frying pan. Fry until the underneath is lightly browned and crisp. Snip the stems off with a pair of scissors and turn over to fry the other side. Meanwhile, reheat the sauce if you wish. When the elderflower fritters have browned, lift them out of the pan and drain briefly on kitchen paper. Serve immediately, scattered with a touch of sugar and drizzled generously with the vanilla ruby sauce. Repeat with the remaining elderflowers.

Seasonal produce

Turn a restricted budget into a positive asset by basing meals around the best seasonal produce, which is usually far cheaper than unseasonal imports. The following paragraphs list some of the most affordable seasonal offerings, to give you an idea of what to look out for.

Summer (June, July, August)

Vegetables: broad beans, peas, courgettes, tomatoes, aubergines, runner beans, carrots, cauliflower, cucumbers, green beans, runner beans, lettuces, corn on the cob, red and green peppers, chillies, new potatoes, radishes, spinach, new-season turnips and beetroot.

Herbs: herbs of all kinds are at their most prolific in summer but if you have your own garden, or a sunny windowsill, make a point of growing basil, tarragon, marjoram, dill and mint. If you are lucky, the elderflower season will overlap for a week or so with the first gooseberries – use the flowers to flavour gooseberry fool or jam.

Fruit: strawberries, gooseberries, raspberries, loganberries, tayberries, black, white and redcurrants, cherries, blueberries, grapes. Then in August, apricots, plums, melons, greengages, peaches, nectarines, Discovery apples.

Meat and fish: mackerel, sardines, squid, whitebait, herring, plaice.

Autumn (September, October, November)

Vegetables: celeriac, marrows, winter squashes – including pumpkins, onion squashes, red kuri, crown prince and more – wild mushrooms, parsnips, large main-crop beetroot, potatoes, carrots, cabbages, including the first of the Savoys and early Brussels sprouts, cauliflowers, chard, celery, leeks, onions, swedes, turnips.

Herbs: If you garden, use up the last of the sorrel and put lovage into marvellous warming soups. Sage, thyme and rosemary come into their own in cold-weather dishes, while mint provides a lingering note of freshness.

Fruit: blackberries, autumn raspberries, the last of the plums (especially damsons), elderberries, grapes, apples, pears, quinces if you can beg them from somebody with a tree, and likewise crab-apples, new-season nuts – in particular chestnuts and wet walnuts, followed by milky fresh filberts and cobnuts; the first helping of cranberries in time for Thanksgiving at the end of November. Seasonal citrus fruits creep in.

Meat and fish: the game season is really getting going now, and prices drop towards the end of November as winter looms. Partridge and pheasant in particular are phenomenal value, especially if you are prepared to pluck or skin them. Prime cuts of venison are expensive, but other cuts that are less in demand, such as shoulder, can be had for a song. Rabbit, wild or domesticated, is just the ticket for warming stews and casseroles. Cod, coley, conger eel, herring, ling, mussels, plaice, skate, whiting, witch.

Winter (December, January, February)

Vegetables: leeks, beetroot, Brussels sprouts, Brussels tops, cauliflower, red, white and winter green cabbages, Savoy cabbages, celeriac, parsnips, potatoes, carrots, Jerusalem artichokes, curly kale, watercress, winter squashes, kohlrabi, onions, swedes, turnips.

Herbs: parsley can survive the cold if the weather is not too severe. If you grow your own herbs, rosemary, thyme and sage will be usable right through winter, needing only minimal protection from the elements – too much rain, rather than cold, is what upsets them most.

Fruit: citrus fruits of all kinds but particularly clementines, satsumas and the host of small oranges, Seville oranges, lemons, limes, the first flush of blood oranges, cranberries, forced rhubarb, apples, pears, pomegranates, bananas, Brazil nuts, chestnuts, coconuts, walnuts.

Meat and fish: the last and often cheapest game in the run up to 1 February, which is the end of the season for most game. As in autumn, pheasant and partridge tend to be the cheapest, especially if you pluck or skin them yourself. Casseroling may be a better bet than roasting in late January. Rabbit is still well worth trying, and cheaper cuts of venison make superb casseroles. Cod, coley, conger eel, flounder, herring, huss, lemon sole, ling, mackerel, mussels, plaice, skate, sprats, whiting, witch.

Spring (March, April, May)

Vegetables: beetroot, home-grown new potatoes (even Jersey Royals are relatively cheap by late May), new-season carrots, spring cabbages, spring greens, watercress, spinach, cauliflowers, radishes, purple sprouting broccoli, and white sprouting broccoli in March if you live in Leicester. The first British asparagus appears in May, early peas and broad beans towards the end of the month, though they will still be pricy.

Herbs: in gardens, chives will be thrusting forth, as well as sweet cicely (to cook with rhubarb: it dampens the acidity of the rhubarb so you need to add less sugar). Sorrel will be plentiful enough for making soup. Mint is growing fast enough now to grace early new potatoes and other new-season vegetable treats. Towards the end of May the first creamy elderflowers appear, free for the picking, superb for fritters, cordial, and flavouring all manner of puddings.

Fruit: last of the blood oranges and other citrus fruit, loquats, garden rhubarb, bananas; pineapples may still prove good value.

Meat and fish: spring lamb. Mussels can be good value in March and early April, the last month with an 'r' in it for some time; conger eel, flounder, huss, mackerel, lemon sole, whitebait, witch.

A Handful of *Useful* Addresses

Gathered here are the addresses of places that we visited when filming, or that are mentioned in the text.

Kent

Perry Court Farm Shop/Perry Court Pick-Your-Own Farm
Perry Court, Canterbury Road, Bilting, Ashford, Kent TN25 4ES
Telephone 01233 812302

A large farm shop selling an enormous range of fruit and vegetables, as well as local free-range eggs, good cheeses and many other items, including pick-your-own soft fruit in the summer.

Ripple Farm
Crondale, Kent T4 7EB
Telephone 01227 730898

An impressive organic box scheme: for £5, each member gets an excellent weekly selection of organically grown fruit and vegetables including, in summer, some of the choicest salad greens I've seen in ages.

St Augustine's Fish Supplies
Harbour Front, Whitstable, Kent
Telephone 01227 771245

Right by the water's edge, this vast hangar of a fishmonger's sells local fish in prime condition at very good prices. They also smoke some of their own fish on the premises.

Devon

Barnstaple Pannier Market

Every Friday in the town centre, accessible from Butcher's Row and the High Street.

Passmore's Fishmongers
33 Butcher's Row, Barnstaple, Devon EX31 1BW
Telephone 01271 343677

Venton Dairy
Golflinks Road, Westward Ho!
Devon EX39 1HH
Telephone 01237 474244

Sells clotted cream by mail order. Also available from Barnstaple pannier market.

Roly's Fudge Pantry
28 Guildhall Arches, High Street, Barnstaple, Devon EX31 1BL

also at 52 Fore Street, Totnes, Devon TQ9 5RJ
and 12 The Quay, Ilfracombe, Devon EX34 9EQ (Fudge can be sent by post from the Ilfracombe branch: Telephone 01271 867373.)

Real old-fashioned fudge that is made in small batches on the premises, and has that proper melt-in-the-mouth, velvety consistency that most commercial fudge lacks.

Marwood Gardens
Marwood Hill, Barnstaple, Devon EX31 4EB
Telephone 01271 375000

Beautiful gardens tumbling down the slope of the hill that the charming village of Marwood is perched on. Open daily from dawn to dusk, but the plant sales area has the more restricted opening hours of 11am–5pm. (Sunday cream teas are available from the Marwood Church hall.)

Brixton

Electric Avenue Market
Electric Avenue and surrounding streets, London SW2

A vibrant, bustling market for Caribbean foods and other items. Look out for the fish and scarily hot Scotch bonnet chillies.

Northern Ireland

Moyallon Foods
The Farm, 76 Crowhill Road, Craigavon, County Armagh BT66 7AT
Telephone 01762 349100

The first time I met Jilly Acheson of Moyallon Foods she was swinging a brace of pheasant from one hand as she strode through Norah Brown's vegetable garden, but most of the time she is to be found here at Moyallon Foods. It sells rare-breed meats, hams, venison and other high-quality free-range meat and meat products.

Grange Lodge
Grange Road, Dungannon, County Tyrone BT71 7EJ
Telephone 01868 784212
Fax 01868 723891
Contacts: Norah and Ralph Brown

Possibly the best guesthouse in Ireland, run by the wonderful, welcoming Browns. Their hospitality is legendary, the food superb and the rooms are cosy.

Leicester

Sharmilee's Sweet Mart and Restaurant
71–73 Belgrave Road, Leicester LE4 6AS
Telephone 0116 266 8471/
0116 261 0503

Downstairs is the magical, spick and span shop of delights, packed full of all manner of scented, colourful sweetmeats and divine savoury snacks. Upstairs is a smart vegetarian restaurant which serves some cracking food – don't miss the outstanding panir fritters.

The Market
Market Place, Leicester

This has a fabulous range of fruit and vegetables, including a wealth of high-quality exotica at remarkable prices. There's a superb spice stall near the Corn Exchange Pub. If you are lucky enough to visit in March, don't miss the fabulous white sprouting broccoli.

The Curry Club
PO Box 7, Haslemere, Surrey GU27 1EP
Telephone 01428 658327

You can buy vark (edible gold or silver leaf) by mail order from The Curry Club, as well as other Indian ingredients.

Index

Agro dolce date sauce 93
Anchovies, potato pizza with mascarpone, rocket and 40–1
Angel food cake 64
Apples: blackberry and apple compote 65
  compote of apples and raisins 85
  golden Eve's pudding 76–7
Apricots: fried apricots with almonds 113
  rice salad with apricots 21
Asparagus: scrambled eggs with asparagus tips and horseradish 152
  velouté d'asperges 154

Bacon, broad bean and oven-dried tomato salad 28–9
Bananas: banana bread pudding 120
  banana teabread 120–1
Bannock, treacle and sultana 78–9
Barley and mushroom risotto 137
Beef: daube with cannellini beans and rosemary 116–17
  spaghetti and meatballs 132–3
Beetroot: deep-fried leek and beetroot shreds 73–6
  Kumar's beetroot curry 14
  loud mash 73
Betty Skelly's chocolate cake 37
Betty Skelly's coffee cake 37
Bhajis, onion and almond 92
Biscuits, lace 46–7
Blackberry and apple compote 65
Boozy marmalade 124
Bread: banana bread pudding 120
  naan bread with coriander pesto 99
  soda farls 78
  summer pudding 19–20
  treacle and sultana soda bannock 78–9
Brightside baked potatoes 90
Broad bean, oven-dried tomato and bacon salad 28–9
Brown sugar lemonade 56
Butter, herb 96–7

Cakes: angel food cake 64
  Betty Skelly's chocolate cake 37
  Betty Skelly's coffee cake 37
  Greek honey syrup cake 143–4
  Louise's lime and ginger birthday cake 103
  Margaret Pover's moist lemon cake 36–7
  orange torta 140–1
Cannellini beans, daube of beef with 116–17
Caramel: caramelized oranges 117
  rice pudding brûlée 108
Cardamom coconut jelly 102
Carrots: carrot and raisin salad 131
  glazed turnips and carrots 108
  Kumar's Sri Lankan carrot salad 18
  roast carrot salad 119
  spiced carrot and garlic chutney 81
Cheese: Fiona's spinach and feta pie 130
  Goat's cheese pastry 112
  Norah's cheese and chutney purses 71–2
Chicken: Brightside baked potatoes 90

chicken and tarragon patties 152–3
chicken stock 154
devilled drumsticks 118–19
fricassée chicken 58–9
Kenneth's chicken Abigail 20–1
seared chicken and peach sandwich 29–32
Chicken liver and spinach pancakes 145–8
Chickpea mash, garlicky 84–5
Chocolate: Betty Skelly's chocolate cake 37
  le progrés au chocolat 38
Chutney: Norah's cheese and chutney purses 71–2
  spiced carrot and garlic chutney 81
Coconut milk 18–19
  cardamom coconut jelly 102
Coffee cake, Betty Skelly's 37
Coley: fish soup with fennel seeds and chives 145
  Raj fishcakes 45
Coriander: naan bread with coriander pesto 99
  spring onion and coriander mayonnaise 46
Cranberries: pear and cranberry oat crisp 105
Cucumber: mint, grape and cucumber raita 98
  Sri Lankan cucumber sambal 14
Curries: curried pheasant chowder 70–1
  Kumarís beetroot curry 14
Custard 65

Damson sauce for the freezer 80–1
Date sauce, agro dolce 93
La daube dizef 13–14
Devilled drumsticks 118–19

Eggs: custard 65
  la daube dizef 13–14
  scrambled eggs with asparagus tips 152
  tortilla 17–18
Elderberry jelly 80
Elderflower fritters 156
Escoveitched red snapper 53–6
Eve's pudding, golden 76–7

Fiona's spinach and feta pie 130
Fish soup with fennel seeds and chives 145
Fishcakes, Raj 45
Fricassée chicken 58–9
Fritters, elderflower 156
Fruit: summer pudding 19–20

Garlic: garlic jam 84–5
  spiced carrot and garlic chutney 81
  Tatin of caramelized onions and garlic 112
  wild garlic mash 143
Giardiniera 49
Golden Eve's pudding 76–7
Greek honey syrup cake 143–4

Hazelnuts: le progrés au chocolat 38
Herbs 7–8
  herb butter 96–7
Honey syrup cake, Greek 143–4

Ice-cream: lemon mascarpone 41
  mango and lime kulfi 101

Jam: garlic jam 84–5

plum and walnut jam 48
Jam jars, sterilizing 124
Jelly: cardamom coconut 102
  elderberry 80
  rhubarb and orange 153–4

Kenneth's chicken Abigail 20–1
Kulfi, mango and lime 101
Kumar's beetroot curry 14
Kumar's Sri Lankan carrot salad 18

Lace biscuits 46–7
Lamb: nettle and tomato bredy 142
  rosemary and garlic lamb chops 84–5
Leeks: deep-fried leek and beetroot shreds 73–6
  poor man's asparagus 106–7
Lemon: brown sugar lemonade 56
  lemon mascarpone ice-cream 41
  Margaret Pover's moist lemon cake 36–7
Lettuce: buttered lettuce with cumin and lemon 140
Lime: escoveitched red snapper 53–6
  Louise's lime and ginger birthday cake 103
Loud mash 73
Louise's lime and ginger birthday cake 103

Mackerel, grilled fillets with feisty rhubarb relish 155
Mango and lime kulfi 101
Margaret Pover's moist lemon cake 36–7
Marmalade, boozy 124
Marrow: potato and marrow soup 57–8
Masala mushy peas 93
Mayonnaise 28
  spring onion and coriander 46
Meatballs: polpettone con formaggio 104–5
  spaghetti, meatballs and no-meatballs 132–3
Meringues: le progrés au chocolat 38
Mint, grape and cucumber raita 98
Mushroom and pearl barley risotto 137
Mussels with tomato, basil and garlic 26–7

Naan bread with coriander pesto 99
Nettles: nettle and tomato bredy 142
  nettle soup 129–30
Norah's baked pears with amaretti biscuits 71
Norah's cheese and chutney purses 71–2

Oats: lace biscuits 46–7
  pear and cranberry oat crisp 105
Onions: nettle and tomato bredy 142
  onion and almond bhajis 92
  onion cachumber 100
  onion marmalade 152–3
  roast roots and alliums with tamarind 97
  Tatin of caramelized onions and garlic 112
Oranges: boozy marmalade 124
  caramelized oranges 117
  orange torta 140–1
  rhubarb and orange jelly 153–4
  Seville orange curd 125

Pancakes, chicken liver and spinach 145–8
Panzanella, Umbrian 44–5
Pastries: Norah's cheese and chutney purses 71–2
Pastry, goat's cheese 112

Peaches: seared chicken and peach
    sandwich 29–32
Pearl barley and mushroom risotto 137
Pears: Norah's baked pears with amaretti
    biscuits 71
    pear and cranberry oat crisp 105
Peas: masala mushy peas 93
Peppers Sorrento 26
Pesto, coriander 99
Pheasant: curried pheasant chowder 70–1
    pan-fried breasts 72–3
    pheasant stock 70
    skinning 66–8
Pie, Fiona's spinach and feta 130
Pigeon peas: rice and peas 59
Pineapple, roast with butterscotch sauce 133
Pinzimonio 39–40
Pizza: potato pizza with anchovies,
    mascarpone and rocket 40–1
Plaice: battered plaice and herb sandwich
    15–16
Plums: plum and walnut jam 48
    roast plums with clotted cream 32
Polpettone con formaggio 104–5
Poor man's asparagus 106–7
Pork: polpettone con formaggio 104–5
    Walter's jerk pork 58
Potatoes: Brightside baked potatoes 90
    la daube dizef 13–14
    griddled potato, tomato and red onion
    salad 16
    loud mash 73
    potato and marrow soup 57–8
    potato pizza with anchovies, mascarpone
    and rocket 40–1
    Raj fishcakes 45
    shoestring chips 27
    tortilla 17–18
    wild garlic mash 143
Le progrés au chocolat 38
Pumpkin, sweetcorn and sweet potato stew
    60–1

Raita, mint, grape and cucumber 98
Raj fishcakes 45
Raspberry sorbet 46
Red cabbage, orange and black olive salad
    113
Red snapper, escoveitched 53–6
Relishes: feisty rhubarb 155
    tomato and runner bean 48–9
Rhubarb: feisty rhubarb relish 155
    rhubarb and orange jelly 153–4
Rice: rice and peas 59
    rice pudding brûlée 108
    rice salad with apricots 21
Roast carrot salad 119
Runner bean and tomato relish 48–9

Salads: broad bean, oven-dried tomato and
    bacon 28–9
    carrot and raisin 131
    griddled potato, tomato and red onion 16
    Kumar's Sri Lankan carrot 18
    red cabbage, orange and black olive 113
    rice with apricots 21
    roast carrot 119
    Umbrian panzanella 44–5
Salmon fillet, seared spiced 96–7
Sandwich, seared chicken and peach 29–32

Sauces: agro dolce date sauce 93
    damson sauce for the freezer 80–1
Scones, Violet Graham's 36
Seasonal produce 6, 157
Seville orange curd 125
Shoestring chips 27
Soda farls 78
Sorbet, raspberry 46
Soups: curried pheasant chowder 70–1
    fish soup with fennel seeds and chives 145
    nettle soup 129–30
    potato and marrow soup 57–8
    velouté d'asperges 154
Spaghetti, meatballs and no-meatballs
    132–3
Spices 7
Spinach: chicken liver and spinach
    pancakes 145–8
    Fiona's spinach and feta pie 130
    stir-fried spinach with cashew nuts,
    currants and south Indian spices 98
Spring onion and coriander mayonnaise 46
Sri Lankan cucumber sambal 14
Starfruit, poached 100
Stock: chicken 154
    pheasant 70
Summer pudding 19–20
Sweetcorn, pumpkin and sweet potato stew
    60–1

Tamarind, roast roots and alliums with 97
Tatin of caramelized onions and garlic 112
Teabread, banana 120–1
Tofu: spaghetti and no-meatballs 132–3
Tomatoes: la daube dizef 13–14
    griddled potato, tomato and red onion
    salad 16
    mussels with tomato, basil and garlic 26–7
    nettle and tomato bredy 142
    oven-dried tomatoes 29
    spaghetti, meatballs and no-meatballs
    132–3
    tomato and runner bean relish 48–9
Tortilla 17–18
Treacle and sultana soda bannock 78–9
Turkey schnitzel 107
Turnips and carrots, glazed 108

Umbrian panzanella 44–5

Vegetables: giardiniera 49
    pinzimonio 39–40
    roast roots and alliums with tamarind 97
Velouté d'asperges 154
Violet Graham's scones 36

Walnuts: plum and walnut jam 48
Walter's jerk pork 58

Yoghurt: mint, grape and cucumber raita 98